One *of* thousands, this book is donated to the Roesch Library by Laila and Robert Werner, a graduate *of* the class *of* 1936

*This gift is dedicated
to the memory of
Robert Reiling,
a classmate and dear friend*

"A good book is the precious lifeblood of a master spirit, embalmed and treasured up on purpose to a life beyond life." — *Milton*

Children of Poverty

Studies and Dissertations on
the Effects of Single Parenthood,
the Feminization of Poverty,
and Homelessness

Stuart Bruchey
UNIVERSITY OF MAINE
General Editor

A Garland Series

The Social Reality of a Group of Rural, Low-Status, Appalachian Women

A Grounded Theory Study

Judith Ivy Fiene

Garland Publishing, Inc.
New York & London
1993

Copyright © 1993 by Judith Ivy Fiene
All rights reserved

Library of Congress Cataloging-in-Publication Data

Fiene, Judith Ivy, 1936–
  The social reality of a group of rural, low-status, Appalachian women : a grounded theory study / Judith Ivy Fiene.
    p. cm. — (Children of poverty)
  Thesis (Ph.D.) —
  ISBN 0-8153-1116-8 (alk. paper)
  1. Rural women—Tennessee—Cocke County. 2. Poor women—Tennessee—Cocke County. 3. Women—Tennessee—Cocke County—Social conditions. 4. Cocke County (Tenn.) Rural conditions. I. Title. II. Series
HQ1438.T2F54   1993
305.42'09768'895—dc20   92-40120
                                                              CIP

Printed on acid-free, 250-year-life paper
Manufactured in the United States of America

This work is dedicated to my parents, Randolph Wilson Ivy and Tressa Kaercher Ivy

CONTENTS

Preface — ix

Chapter 1: CONCEPTUAL FRAMEWORK — 3

Statement of Problem — 5
The Social Construction of Reality — 7
Social Stratification — 8
Nominalist Perspective of Class/Status — 9
Appalachian Region — 10
Self-Concept — 12
Summary — 12

Chapter 2: SOCIAL STATUS AND FAMILY PATTERNS — 15

Social Status and Social Reality — 15
Life Patterns in Low-Status Groups — 17
Rural Life Patterns — 20
Poverty in Rural Appalachia — 22
Social Stratification in Appalachia — 27
Low-Status Appalachian Women — 28

Chapter 3: RESEARCH METHODS — 31

Study Site — 32
Selection of Participants — 34
Data Analysis — 36
Limitations of the Study — 39

Chapter 4: FAMILY ROLES AND EXPECTATIONS   41

Female Roles   42
Male Roles   51
Male-Female Relationships   54
Role Failures   57
Socialization to World Outside of Family   58
Summary   60

Chapter 5: SOCIAL RELATIONSHIPS   61

Awareness of Social Status   61
Interactional Expectations   64
Dealing with Feeling Put-Down   69
Discussion   70

Chapter 6: FEELINGS ABOUT SELF   73

Self-Esteem and Family Role Performance   74
Negative Feelings About Self   76
Endurance and the Little Things in Life   78
Summary   81

Chapter 7: SUMMARY AND IMPLICATIONS   83

Summary of Findings   83
Implications   86

Appendix   89
References   91
Index   101

Preface

The present study of Appalachian women has come out of a long-standing interest in rural family life in East Tennessee. A native of Louisville, Kentucky, I considered myself an urbanite when in 1975 I moved with my family to Knoxville, Tennessee. My prior experience with rural families had been as a social worker in Southern Indiana with rural and small-town parents who brought their developmentally disabled children to specialty medical clinics sponsored by the Crippled Children's Program, a division of the State Department of Public Welfare.

My first employment in Knoxville was as a psychiatric social worker at the regional state mental hospital where patients were assigned to different wards, not on the basis of diagnosis, but depending on the county from which they came. This was my first clue that attachment to and identification with one's place of origin is of paramount importance in East Tennessee. After I became more accustomed to the accents and speech patterns of my clients and their families, I began to believe that life in their rural counties was in some ways different from rural Indiana. I was frustrated because hospital policy keep me confined to the facility and made no provisions for visits to local communities.

Within a year I took a position at the Birth Defects Center, University of Tennessee Medical Center, Knoxville (now the Developmental and Genetic Center). This position called for field work with families in their homes and communities to assist them in dealing with the needs of their disabled children. Thus for eight years I was able to enter the homes of largely poor, rural families and observe how they lived. I also had regular contacts with teachers of special education, public health workers, and human services providers. I became particularly sensitive to the vast differences in my view of life as a college-educated, city-bred, feminist and the lives of most of the women

I met in the course of my work. I talked with women who lived in rough, inadequate houses and shared their couches with the chickens who came in the unscreened doors and windows. I sat around wood burning stoves in rooms so stuffy and so full of people, pets, and beds, that the oxygen supply seemed totally inadequate. I saw women in neat but crowded trailers living in almost complete isolation. I drove up hollows that were, to my surprise, still full of ice a week after all other roads were clear. I wanted to record all of my observations somehow but my job allowed me no time to examine my experiences systematically.

Acceptance into the University of Tennessee doctoral program in social work in 1983 finally gave me the opportunity to explore my interest in Appalachian society. I found the popular images and tales regarding the Appalachian people to be inadequate in describing my observations of life in the southern mountains. I discovered that much more had been published about the Appalachian past and its folkways than about its present. It was then that I first read *The Roots of Futility* by Polansky, Borgman, and DeSaix (1972), one of the few available texts on parenting, particularly mothering, in low-income, Appalachian families. The authors' descriptions of rural living conditions were identical with the circumstances of some of the families I had observed, and their depictions of inadequate mothers and dysfunctional families did fit a small number of families. But I became concerned that readers would take these portraits as the only reality, if only because the findings of Polansky et al. unfortunately seem to confirm many of the hillbilly stereotypes.

My goal then became to design a research study that would add to the store of knowledge about rural Appalachian families, particularly low-income women and their children. I believe strongly that social class is a primary factor in determining family life-styles and child-rearing patterns. My own experience growing up in a working-class family with middle-class aspirations had sensitized me to the ease with which higher status persons make assumptions about those lower on the status scale. This takes the form of concluding that behaviors observed within a social class have the same meaning to outside observers as to the participants. Such assumptions may be so accepted as popular wisdom that they permeate research questions and

Preface

methods. In an effort to deal with my own cultural assumptions, I decided to become a "visiting anthropologist" in my own culture and approach study participants as the experts who alone understand the socially-constructed meanings upon which are built the habits of their daily lives. I was fortunate to have available in my university professors knowledgeable in the use of grounded theory and ethnographic methods who gave me the research tools that made this study possible. As a preliminary step in learning to process qualitative data, I conducted an observation study of family behaviors in a public health clinic setting.

I choose for the site of my dissertation research a rural county which I had visited almost weekly during my years with the Birth Defects Center. My familiarity with the geography and with personnel in the human services shortened my entry time into the study proper. I was also conversant with local speech habits and idioms. Without such prior knowledge, a study of this type would undoubtedly take longer than the five months I spent in residence. Although I carried a tape recorder in my car, I decided almost immediately that using the recorder during my home visits would be intrusive and might induce more formal or self-conscious responses. I wanted to encourage an atmosphere where the participants felt free to put forward their ideas and views. Small children in the households were usually in and out of the room during my visits, expecting some attention from the visitor, and not infrequently climbing up to sit on my lap. Audio taping such visits would have been awkward at best. Consequently, I used the tape recorder immediately after leaving a home visit to record my observations.

Since the completion of this study I have presented my findings at conferences both outside the region and within it. The type of positive feedback I have received from conference participants who are native to Appalachia leads me to believe that the family role profiles I have delineated are also applicable to at least some families in more middle-class circumstances. My most recent research studies have focused on the lives of battered women in this region.

The findings in any ethnographic study are usually rich, colorful, and detailed. Because such findings interest us at a personal as well as professional level it is tempting to interpret the conclusions has having a wider applicability than may be warranted. This study concentrates on 18 women in 14 families. What is needed are more studies that examine the experiences, beliefs, and behaviors of members of low-status families. I hope that those who undertake such studies will respect, as

I have tried to do, the integrity and strength of these rural mountain families whose lives have been shaped by economic forces largely beyond their control.

ACKNOWLEDGMENTS

I wish to express my appreciation to my doctoral committee members, Dr. A. Elfin Moses, chairperson, Dr. Jerry Cates, Dr. David Harrison, and Dr. Margaret Wheeler, for their advice and support during the course of my research and the writing of the dissertation. I am also grateful for the assistance or Dr. Catherine Faver, Dr. Gary Peterson, and Dr. David Austin in the preparation of my research proposal. Dr. Robert Bonovich was a source of help and encouragement during my first year in the doctoral program.

This research would not have been possible without the help of my many friends in Cocke County, Tennessee. The staff of the Cocke County Child Health and Development Project, Gaynell Proffitt, Donna Bundy, Debrorah Stokely, and Judy Neese, provided a welcome stopping place at their office. They were always ready to listen to my ideas and encourage my efforts. Brenda Smith was also generous with her time and insights. My friends, Lois Kenyon and Leala Balch, were always helpful and it was through them I met the perfect landlady, Viola Clark. Kristen Roberts-Ball and Dianne Levy read part of the manuscript and gave me valuable feedback. I appreciate the opportunity afforded me by Judy Chobanian and her staff to do volunteer work with the food distribution program at the Community Action Agency. They made me feel welcome. Harold Cates, Director of the Cocke County Department of Human Services, and members of his staff were always helpful when I called on them.

I will always be grateful to the women who participated in this study. Although I cannot name them, all names have been changed, I will never forget these women who were so trusting, so generous with their time, and so hospitable.

And finally I want to recognize my husband, Dr. Donald Mark Fiene, and my children, Karen Ivy Fiene and Bruce Marcus Fiene. I have been fortunate to have their love, support, and encouragement.

The Social Reality of a Group of Rural, Low-Status, Appalachian Women

CHAPTER ONE

CONCEPTUAL FRAMEWORK

Chronic poverty and the stigma associated with low social status are important factors in structuring the social worlds of low-income Appalachians. This is not a recent phenomenon. The once self-sufficient economy of Appalachia, founded on family-based subsistence farming and independent commodity production, was gradually eroded by the capitalistic market economy, which made its first inroads into urban areas in the nineteenth century, and gradually spread into rural areas.

The Second World War initiated a period of national economic growth and brought about the rapid expansion of the mining industry and manufacturing enterprises, such as textile factories, in Appalachia. This moved much of the rural population into the wage labor market (Eller, 1979; Precourt, 1983). But this exploitation of the region's resources, mineral and human, did not secure a viable regional economy, and during times of economic recession Appalachians migrated to the industrial cities of mid-America seeking employment. More recent industrial relocations to Third World countries have led to the closing of many of the area's mines and mills.

The indigenous people remaining in the region have consistently been paid wages that lag behind national averages and have suffered higher poverty levels. Although 9.6% of all American families live in poverty, 15.6% of the rural families living in the Appalachian counties of Kentucky, West Virginia, Virginia, North Carolina, and Tennessee live below the poverty line. A significant number of the female-headed families with children in the United States (40.3%) and in rural Appalachia (44.2%) live in poverty, with annual incomes below $7356 for a family of four (Tickamyer & Tickamyer, 1987b).

Images of Appalachian poverty have been plentiful. Precourt (1983) shows that such images have their source in the labeling of

Appalachians as deprived or as displaying antisocial traits, the labeling of subsistence farming as unproductive, and the denigration of local culture as a rationale for exploitation. The media have been active in perpetuating stereotypical images of low-income Appalachians in television documentaries, entertainment shows, and cartoons (Newcomb, 1979).

These images of the poor in Appalachia are often tied implicitly to the belief that the lifestyles of the poor are responsible for their continued impoverishment. This view was advanced by observers using a culture-of-poverty model and has been an indirect source for many of the stereotypes associated with Appalachian poverty (Photiadis, n.d.; Weller, 1965). This model hypothesizes that individual adaptations to the circumstances of poverty are transmitted to progeny who repeat self-defeating behaviors thus perpetuating the cycle of disadvantage (Lewis, 1966).

Despite sound critiques of this perspective (Leacock, 1971; Valentine, 1968), many researchers have persisted in seeking the causes of continued social problems in the life styles of low-status families. This perspective also appears in the rhetoric of the current conservative administration, which blames financial assistance programs for creating dysfunctional family life styles (Murray, 1984).

The stereotypical images of the poor in Appalachia and the more general stigma associated with living in poverty in America create a devalued social role and low social status for the many Appalachian women whose incomes are below the poverty mark (Waxman, 1977). Occupying this stigmatized position can result in negative or defensive feelings about self when the low-status person engages in interactions with higher status individuals (Sennett & Cobb, 1973). Thus the social world of rural, low-status Appalachian women is bounded by stereotyped images of Appalachians and prejudices toward low-status individuals, just as their economic world is bounded by limited economic opportunities and sparse resources.

Conceptual Framework　　　　　　　　　　　　　　　　　　　　5

Statement of the Problem

The purpose of this study is to discover how rural, low-status, Appalachian women perceive their social world. The initial scope of this study is proposed in broad terms in order to allow the respondents to determine which aspects of their social world they consider to be important and to avoid the imposition of any preconceptions by the researcher. How the women view their world and how they are conceptualized by others is important to social work because these women and their children are among the primary clients of health and welfare agencies and are the recipients of resources from multiple state and federal programs. Social workers offer services to these individuals and families and participate in the program planning and policy making that affect the women's life circumstances. A deeper understanding of this client group should enhance social work helping efforts.

As a group, low-status, rural Appalachian women have not been the subject of much scientific investigation. There has been little systematic attention given to the importance of gender in determining individual life courses in Appalachia (Tickamyer & Tickamyer, 1987a; Walls & Billings, 1977). There is a paucity of statistical data regarding Appalachian women, in general, and practically no data on female-headed households (Weeks, 1980). Analyses of social structure in Appalachian communities frequently define women's lives solely in relation to their role functions or position within the traditional family group (Photiadis, 1986; Stephenson, 1968; Schwarzweller, Brown, & Mangalam, 1971).

Discussions of Appalachian women in the majority of ethnographic and sociological studies are embedded in analyses and descriptions of the family. Citing the prevalence of familism in the region (Heller & Quesada, 1977), these studies concentrate their attention either on the kinship network or the family of procreation. However, low-status women may be labeled in their rural communities in terms of the often derogatory reputation attached to their kinship group, or they may be categorized as members of families that adhere to traditional mountain values.

Information regarding low-status Appalachians in general has consisted largely of impressionistic accounts of mountain life (Kephart, 1984), studies that compare the ways of mountain families with the implicit or explicit norms of urban, nuclear families (Weller, 1965), or studies describing character disorders said to be prevalent in this group (Looff, 1971). Although these studies are useful in enumerating the problems created by poverty, they present a perspective from the outside looking in. Missing from these portrayals of the lives of low-status women is an appreciation of their view of reality and of the adaptive strengths that have enabled the women to cope with life's vicissitudes.

Qualitative Methodology

This study of low-status women utilizes qualitative methods, unstructured interviews and participant observation, to obtain the women's reflections on their past and current life concerns. The analysis of these data using the grounded theory method has allowed the researcher to ascertain the women's interpretations of the social processes that structure their social world.

Research efforts that utilize grounded theory to examine their data are not guided by the theories and hypotheses that are the foundation of hypothetico-deductive research. Rather the concepts pertinent to grounded theory research are derived from observations of a social situation, and the theories that best explain the observed social interactions are constructed from these concepts. Ideally, grounded theory researchers do not read the literature of the area prior to the initiation of their project nor try to predict the outcomes of their analysis. They do not construct a research design nor identify dependent variables.

It is short-sighted, however, to assume that researchers using grounded theory enter the field with no presuppositions, opinions, or even hunches. As products of their culture, scientists are bound by the values and beliefs current in their society, and their perspectives are always informed by their experience and expert knowledge (Keller, 1985).

Conceptual Framework 7

The author of this study has been influenced both by her past experience in interacting with low-status people and by the particular conceptual frameworks that have helped structure her understanding of her own social world. Most pertinent to this study are the concepts of the social construction of reality, social stratification, and the nominalist perspective on class/status.

The Social Construction of Reality

The concept of the social construction of reality has been developed by Berger and Luckmann (1967). They conclude that social reality is not a single, knowable, objective quantity but a socially constructed feature of a relativistic world. They conjecture that individuals project their mental constructs, derived from the empirical data of their subjective experiences, onto the external world and reach a consensus of opinion, with others in their social group, that is labeled *reality*. Individuals are inducted into this agreed-upon-world through their socialization as children. The immutable facts of this world are dictated by their physical environment and the social structure and institutions of their specific society.

The social context into which one is born determines the content of one's thoughts. Whereas individual differences in personality result from the variables of intelligence, temperament, and experience, the mental constructs by which one interprets thoughts, feelings, and experiences are derived from one's culture (Shutz, 1962). Primary socialization during childhood is the initial induction into one's position in the social world as provided by parents and other caretakers.

This perspective is further elaborated in symbolic interactionist theory, which hypothesizes that the child's concept of self is formed from the characteristics that are imputed to the child by significant others, usually family members. The family's world view, including the implications of their perceived position in it, is internalized by the young child. Patterns of child rearing in all cultures have an adaptive component reflecting environmental contingencies, past and present, that have been integrated into the group's belief system (Levine, 1977).

Reflecting the family's position in the larger social structure, parents create a world for their children that contains the symbols and concepts reflecting that position. The family life style, including values, beliefs, and use of language, is derived from the cultural store available to specific parents. This perception may later be challenged, either during secondary socialization (which occurs, for example, in the educational process) or in adult life, but individuals will erect tenacious defenses to preserve their initial view of reality (Peterson & Rollins, 1987).

Social Stratification

People born into a low socio-economic group are especially vulnerable to the stigmatizing process of the stratification system. Sennett and Cobb (1973) point out that in American society to stand out from the crowd, to be somebody, is the source of personal dignity.

> The possibility of failure is the most uncomfortable phenomenon in American life. There is no room for failure in our schemes of respect. . . . There is, as well, indifference to those who do not move ahead. Failures and static people . . . are seen as having undeveloped personalities; the uncomfortable feelings about those who do not "make something of themselves" when they have a chance, come out of an assumption that men can be respected only as they become in some way distinctive, as they stand out from the mass. (p. 183)

The belief that all Americans have the opportunity to make something of themselves, obscures the workings of the stratification system operative from birth and internalized during the socialization process. Sennett and Cobb's 1973 study of working-class males in New England documents how the negative assessments of powerful others are accepted by lower-class children. These assessments are integrated into the child's self-image, producing adult respondents who feel personally responsible for their low-status position.

Conceptual Framework 9

Four terms, Appalachian, low-status, rurality, and self-concept, used throughout this study have broad and varied definitions. Following is a discussion of the way in which these terms have been conceptualized in this research.

Nominalist Perspective of Class/Status

The term low-status is used in this study to describe both the economic position of the women discussed and their ascribed social position relative to others in their social world. This approach is based on stratification theory as proposed by Max Weber.

> Weber saw property, power, and prestige as three separate though interacting bases on which hierarchies are created in any society. Property differences generate *classes*; power differences generate *political parties*; and prestige differences generate *status groupings* or strata. (Tumin, 1967:6)

Weber's thesis is evident in the definition of a social class as "a grouping of individuals with similar positions and similar political and economic interests within the stratification system" (Kerbo, 1983:12). The three main criteria for class are taken to be position in the occupational structure (a measure of prestige), position in the authority structure, that is, how many others take orders from one (a measure of power), and ownership of income-producing property (a measure of class). An assumption of this study is that the characteristics of any class or status group, their occupations, educational levels, and power positions will influence their life chances and their share of society's rewards. This perspective has been defined as nominalist (Kerbo, 1983).

These measures of social position produce a scale or hierarchy of status ranging from high to low. Social status, then, is an evaluative concept. Although social status has been developed as an explanatory concept within anthropology and sociology, it is a reification of what already exists in the everyday world. Bernard (1981) notes that social status is a factor in our personal interactions and is largely determined by local custom, attitudes, and values. It is when individuals from different local groups interact that social status becomes significant.

Until recently, women have been relegated to an anomalous position in discussions of social stratification. Most often it has been assumed that married women occupy the same social classes and strata as their spouses. In general, women's social positions have been solely associated with, first, their family of orientation and, later, with their husbands' status positions. Women's work (occupation) within the family has been ignored and their participation in the labor market obscured.

More recently, feminist scholars have suggested that the structure of social class is different for women than for men and has a strong link to the women's reproductive status and perceived economic dependency on men (Bernard, 1981; Petchesky, 1983). Thus a woman's fertility rate and role in the labor market, as well as the occupation of her mate, are factors that determine her social class. This type of categorization does not produce the same type of hierarchical groups as in classical social stratification. In feminist terms, the women in this study can be characterized as belonging to the

> high-fertility, low-labor-force-participation group who are working-class--who never or hardly ever work outside the home and are married to working-class men or receiving welfare. . . . (Petchesky, 1983:232)

Appalachian Region

The most often used definition of the Appalachian region was developed by the Appalachian Regional Commission (ARC), which was created in 1965. The ARC was formed by the governors of the 13 states that contain a portion of Appalachia (Alabama, Georgia, Kentucky, Maryland, Mississippi, New York, North Carolina, Ohio, Pennsylvania, South Carolina, Tennessee, Virginia, and West Virginia). The Commission was set up to study the counties in these states "which had been traditionally weakest in economic development" (Ergood, 1983:35).

Subsequently, this geographical area, which roughly follows the northeast-to-southwest path of the Appalachian mountain chain, was divided into three subregions: Northern, Central, and Southern Appalachia. These subdivisions represent the distribution of more local characteristics such as income, population, and employment patterns

Conceptual Framework

(New Appalachian Subregions, 1974). Cocke County, Tennessee, the site of this research study, is located in the Southern Appalachian region, which stretches from the western panhandle of Virginia, through the mountains of North Carolina and East Tennessee, the northern tip of South Carolina, Georgia, and Alabama, to the northeast counties of Mississippi. Technically speaking, any individual born in that area is an Appalachian.

Rurality

Census-takers have defined rurality in terms of the density of population living in a specific area and the proximity of the population to urban centers, but others recognize that the concept of rurality encompasses factors other than location. Bealer, Willits, and Kuvlesky (1965) suggest that at least three factors contribute to a substantive definition of rurality: the ecological, the occupational, and the socio-cultural. It is important that these factors be considered in conjunction with one another, for taken independently, each aspect of rurality has limited applicability.

Ecologically, the size and density of population may or may not be related to the patterned interactions of the people. Occupational definitions have often been limited to agricultural activities that are becoming less and less a factor in the economic base for rural living in some parts of the United States. Socio-cultural assumptions regarding rural populations have often been ambiguous, dealing sometimes with values and ideals and at others times with behaviors. No current consensus exists on a definition of rurality. However, taken together the ecological, occupational, and socio-cultural status of a population can be used as objective indicators in research.

Lowe and Peek (1974) have defined the rural population in the United States as all farm residents, open county non-farm residents, and residents of areas with populations of fewer than 2500. Urban residence is considered to be in areas with populations of 50,000 or more. In their opinion, the urban/rural status of people living in areas with populations between 2500 and 50,000 is too difficult to define. Using these definitions, Lowe and Peek (1974) found that urban/rural differences in attitude and behavior still exist in our society.

No available definitions of rurality address the conditions that were found in this study. Some of the women in the study currently reside in the county seat, population 8000, but they and their families have lived wherever low-rent housing is available in the county.

The women do not consistently belong to any occupational group other than homemaker, but most have done farm work at some time (stripping tobacco, harvesting tomatoes), and a few have worked in area factories or been motel maids. In terms of population numbers, the rural nature of their county is questionable. But the ecological, occupational, and socio-cultural aspects of their lives make these women rural, in agreement with their own perceptions that they are "country people."

Self-Concept

This study is grounded in women's reflections regarding their interactions with others over their life course. In this narrative process the women reveal images of how they perceive themselves, as well as how they have felt about other's behavior toward them. In so doing, various aspects of their conceptions of self are unveiled.

One of the more accessible and important dimensions of the self-concept is self-appraisal or self-evaluation that is used as the basis for building individual self-esteem. According to Gecas (1982), there are two important aspects of self-esteem, a sense of power and a sense of worth. The first is based on an individual's feelings of efficacy. The second is derived from the norms and values that direct personal and interpersonal behavior, and includes one's sense of justice, reciprocity, and honor.

Summary

Status position in American society is a significant factor in defining reality for individuals and groups in different strata. Individuals from low-status groups have been stereotyped in terms of the ways they are thought to vary from middle-status norms. Increasing the amount of knowledge available regarding low-status individuals' perspectives, what is important in their world views, should be helpful to social work professionals interested in serving these population groups. This point of view is exemplified in social work theory by Howard Goldstein

Conceptual Framework

(1981), who is concerned with the consequences of the larger society's continuing inability to improve the life possibilities of the powerless.

> It is the individual, alone or joined with others, who must have the decisive say at some point about the changes that will affect his life. Social or political action undertaken without regard for this principle often succeeds only in shifting the scenery while the human drama remains unchanged. Of greater risk, such actions may come to convince its presumed beneficiaries that they are indeed incompetent, dependent, and helpless. (p. 9)

This study has been designed to develop a deeper understanding of the social realities of low-status, rural, Appalachian women. Its methodological base is found in phenomenological philosophy, which points to the power of the social context in the construction of social meaning and, ultimately, social reality.

CHAPTER TWO

SOCIAL STATUS AND FAMILY PATTERNS

Two major areas of research provide a background to this study. The first pertains to the relationship between the development of individuals' concepts of social reality and their social status. The second includes investigations of life patterns in low-status groups, that is, family structure and function, group interaction patterns, and general values and beliefs. This chapter will review studies of low-status life patterns, urban-rural differences in life patterns, and characteristics specifically attributed to the people of Appalachia.

Social Status and Social Reality

The theoretical position that an individual's perceptions of social reality are structured or influenced through the processes of early childhood socialization is generally accepted in the literature. However, less agreement exists regarding the role of variables such as social position, ethnicity, and gender in these processes. Two different aspects of this question have been considered. First, how do the values, beliefs, and socialization practices of parents from different class groups differ? Second, how does socialization into a specific social class affect the development of self-concept in children and adults? Underlying all such studies in both categories is the problem of operationalizing the concept of social class. The many different models of class that have been used make comparisons between studies unreliable (Gecas, 1979; Wylie, 1979).

Parental Socialization Practices and Social Class

Variations in parental behaviors among social class groups were the focus of many studies in the 1960s and early 1970s. Areas of behavior addressed in such studies included discipline or child control methods, nature of affectional bonds between parent and child, use of parental power, importance of independence and achievement, and parent-child communication (Bronfenbrenner, 1958; Gecas, 1979; Hess, 1970).

It was found that children in lower-class families were more likely to receive physical punishment for all types of disapproved behavior from an autocratic-style parent. Middle-class children experienced parental use of reasoning or the induction of shame and guilt depending on the type of disapproved behavior. Their parents were more egalitarian in style. Higher socioeconomic status resulted in increased parental involvement and expression of affection with emphasis on recognizing the children's independence and achievements (Gecas, 1979).

Two prominent theorists and researchers in the area of social status and parenting styles are Melvin Kohn and Basil Bernstein. Kohn (1969) takes the position that differences in parental style are the result of characteristic interactions in the parents' occupational settings. The nature of work interactions influence adult beliefs, values, and ideologies. Thus a working-class parent's emphasis on conformity to external standards is seen as reflective of the lack of autonomy in the work place. Kohn's findings are limited, however, by his exclusion of poverty families from his research population and by his concentration on the traditional, intact, nuclear family with a steadily employed father.

Bernstein and Henderson (1973) posit that roles in working-class families are more likely to be position oriented, that is, roles are clearly segregated by status, age, and gender. These family roles are ascribed and rather inflexible. Communication styles in such families are more restricted with emphasis on conformity and concreteness. However, empirical evidence for Bernstein's theory is weak (Gecas, 1979).

Bronfenbrenner (1958) points out that socialization styles also are a function of cultural backgrounds, geographic location, and exposure to culturally current ideologies of child rearing. In his review of twenty-five years of research on the relationship between social class and socialization, Bronfenbrenner (1958) supports the picture of the less flexible lower-class parent who values external controls and conformity to rules. But more recent research contends that there is no more variation in parenting behavior between social classes than there is within a class (Tulkin, 1977).

Development of Self-Concept and Social Class

Efforts have been made to measure the effects on adult self-esteem of perceived differences in personal power and prestige stemming from socioeconomic status. In an extensive review of socioeconomic class and self-concept variables, Wylie (1979) faults the available research for failing to resolve measurement questions important in defining socioeconomic class and failing to explore other possibly relevant variables. He further questions whether better-designed studies would reveal any significant relationship between socioeconomic status and self-regard.

Rosenberg (1979) maintains, however, that a significant correlation exists between levels of education, occupation, and income and self-esteem in adults. Interest in social class as an explanatory variable in socialization research has waned as more attention is directed toward the variables that may mediate social class differences such as biological characteristics of specific gene pools, ethnicity, and the continued socialization process over the life span (Zigler & Seitz, 1978).

Life Patterns in Low-Status Groups

A variety of terms and definitions have been used to label low-status groups. The groups studied have variously been referred to as lower-class, lower-status, low-income, or even working-class. The latter designation arises when the lower class is thought to have at least two levels: the working-class composed of semi-skilled and unskilled laborers at one level and the underemployed or unemployed poor beneath them, with the poverty line taken as a demarcation point (Roach, Gross, & Gursslin, 1969). Other researchers locate working-class or blue-collar workers in the lower-middle class, which includes skilled workers (Levitan, 1971). Yet other writers describe the working-class family as at the bottom of the social spectrum and ignore the world of low-income, single-parent families and welfare recipients

(Lipman-Blumen, 1984). The family is the most frequent unit of observation in all such studies. To the degree possible, the following discussion will be limited to the literature pertaining to the life patterns of individuals and families living below the poverty line (as opposed to the working-class), with particular emphasis on low-status women.

Culture-of-Poverty Theory

A dominant view of the American lower class is represented by writers subscribing to the culture-of-poverty theory (Glazer & Moynihan, 1963; U. S. Department of Labor, 1965). Here the poor are portrayed as participating in a subculture with a unique life style based on common values, attitudes, and behaviors. In this framework, behavioral patterns, originally established as a means of coping with the situational stresses of poverty, are assumed to be counterproductive for upward social mobility. For example, the present-oriented, live-for-today philosophy that is said to be manifested by some of the poor is attributed to their chronic frustration in achieving long-term goals, while at the same time it is blamed for poor work records related to tardiness and absenteeism. These "dysfunctional" behavior patterns are said to be perpetuated through family socialization and thus to doom succeeding generations to continued poverty.

Traits associated with the poor in this perspective include weak egos, lack of impulse control, present-time orientation, desire for immediate gratification, and fatalism. In family life this is said to lead to instability, toleration of deviant behaviors, male domination in white families or matriarchies in black families, early sexual activity, illegitimacy, and female-centered families (Allen, 1970; Kerbo, 1983).

The idea that poor families are different from others in society has thus been taken as an explanation for the continuation of poverty. This literature is replete with descriptions of seriously dysfunctional families (Duberman, 1976; Polansky, Borgman, & DeSaix, 1972). Authors who question the more general application of the culture-of-poverty concept to all low-status people make the caveat that such a theory may apply only to subgroups of the long-term poor such as the poor in Appalachia (Roach & Gursslin, 1969).

The major critiques of the culture-of-poverty theory are that behaviors cannot be taken for values and that even general cultural values are viewed differentially throughout our culture. These criticisms have dislodged this theory from its primacy in the social sciences but have had minimal effect on the public mind and the public view that the poor are responsible for their situation (Gans, 1970; Kerbo, 1983).

Structural Theory

A different perspective on low-status families is offered by qualitative studies that reveal differences between middle-and low-income families in structure and function. These may be viewed, in part, as situational adaptations to the conditions of poverty without implying that the poor are inflexible or resistant to positive changes in their environment (Stack, 1974; Schneider & Smith, 1973). This perspective suggests that the middle class emphasizes the primacy of the self-sufficient nuclear family group, whereas the lower class has a well-organized family system that places value on the flexibility of kinship ties. Lower-class households may include any variety of family members over time with the expectation that kin will reciprocate and lend assistance when needed. Such household elasticity is clearly functional when resources are limited (Schneider & Smith, 1973).

Whatever the household composition, the relationship between mother and children is at the center of low-status family relations, and the mother-adult daughter bond is the most permanent feature of family life (Duberman, 1976; Schneider & Smith, 1973). Abramovitz (1986) points out that low-status women are attempting to fulfill the same family ethic as women in other social classes. The traditional American family ethic "stresses marriage, motherhood, and nonpaid work in the home as the centerpiece of women's role" (p. 214). When fathers are in the home, they are the authority figures and decision-makers.

Men and women have separate social worlds and continue their ties with their own peers and families. Illegitimate children often know who their fathers are and have continuing relationships with his kin. Children are disciplined by physical force rather than by appeals to reason and are taught to be submissive to authority rather than learn to control their own behaviors (Schneider & Smith, 1973).

Low-status women are portrayed as victims of male violence, battered and abused, as well as overworked and self-sacrificial. But they also are viewed as matriarchs wresting family power from their men. The men are authoritarian but not seen as essential to the family, so that a broken marriage does not predict a "broken home." A more personal and detailed view of the life patterns of individual low-income and/or low-status women is to be found in the first-person narratives documented by writers such as Buss (1985) and Coles and Coles (1978). Such documents, however, concentrate on the particular details of each life, and although they increase readers' sensitivity to the individual's life stresses and strains, they provide little information regarding the women's social group.

Characteristics that might seem most applicable to males, particular ethnic groups, or urban dwellers are applied to low-status people in general. Schneider and Smith (1973) state

> ... the lower class tends to place a high premium upon those qualities of the individual which enable him to manipulate circumstances and people, and somehow come out ahead. This requires style, fluent speech, quick wit, and extraordinary personality or innate warmth and 'soul,' rather than the qualities of self discipline which enable the individual to achieve his ends through a long process of training and work. All lower-class groups, irrespective of ethnic origin, place emphasis upon these qualities of manipulation. (p. 58)

It is not at all clear that these qualities would not be valued in other social classes, for example, in the work of stand-up comics and television evangelists. Some would also associate these personality traits with urban rather than rural dwellers. Schneider and Smith (1973) further state that the lower-class person "is indifferent to disapproval of performance, but will react violently to any suggestion that he is 'less than a man'; that is, to an attack upon his attributes as a person" (p. 67).

Rural Life Patterns

As noted above, regardless of social class designation, many writers about the American family appear to use the urban family as the norm for values, beliefs, and behaviors. But normative differences do exist between urban and rural populations. Rural families have changed, but they continue to adhere more closely than urban families to the traditional family norms of our society, with a higher rate of father-headed families and a relatively lower rate of divorce. Rural individuals are also likely to marry earlier, have more children, and share their households with more kin (Brown, 1981).

Rural women appear to be maintaining traditional sex roles as well, citing marriage and children (without full-time outside employment) as their preferred life style. Increases in education and longevity and new family patterns are beginning to offer more choices to rural women. But as Bescher-Donnelly and Smith (1981) point out, the more isolated low-status women with large families have less access to these new role options. When rural women do work outside the home, they are most likely to be employed in lower-paying and lower-status positions. This is due, at least in part, to the limited job opportunities in rural areas.

As a group, rural women have less education than urban women, but often more than rural men. Although more rural individuals are gradually increasing the length of their education, this does not address the inadequacies in the education provided by under-financed rural school systems. Rural women's lack of interest in education has been attributed to their view that it is not germane to their major life-roles as wives and mothers (Bescher-Donnelly & Smith, 1981).

Rural Poor

In the only current description of the characteristics of rural poor families, Fitchen (1981) observes that the stable, intact, family unit is the ideal held by poor couples who believe that such a unit provides the best atmosphere for raising children. She states that parents are dependent on their children to provide self-fulfillment and to enhance their self-image. Couples are also seen to cling together in bad marriages because of their mutual emotional dependence and the fear of losing custody of the children if the family should break up. In addition, women are fearful because of their lack of experience in decision-making and their insecurity outside their home environment.

Emotional problems stemming from their own poverty-stricken childhoods and disrupted families are an important source of stress in the adult lives of low-status persons. Further stress is experienced in the family when they take in, even temporarily, kin who are in need of assistance. Fitchen (1981) believes that poor women are better able to cope with the stress in their lives because they are better able to attain their role ideals as wives and mothers than men who are often frustrated in their roles as providers. In her perspective the poor lack access to secondary social roles in the community, such as PTA president or Boy Scout leader. This deprives the poor of further social resources that might increase their self-esteem. Because Fitchen (1981) does not compare poor rural families with families in other social strata, either rural or urban, it is not clear to what degree the characteristics described above are related to the families' social, economic, and/or geographic positions.

Poverty in Rural Appalachia

Billings (1974) suggests that theories examining poverty in Appalachia can be categorized into those assuming cultural causality and those positing situational explanations. Cultural theorists begin with a concept of Appalachia as a subculture within which low-status families develop a deviant and dysfunctional culture--a culture of poverty--which is transmitted to their children. The mechanism creating this dysfunctional culture may be posited as either a cultural lag--the traditionalist mountaineer out of step with modern, urban society--or as a pattern of regressive personality traits stemming from the inability of some inhabitants to cope with a changing world. This latter point of view has been dominant in social work circles where the assumption of internal causation of behavior holds sway (Polansky et al., 1972).

Theorists looking at situational factors, such as the economic or physical environment, view the characteristics of low-status Appalachians as adaptive behaviors that have survival value. This perspective presents a theoretical base that holds promise for future social work research and practice.

Cultural Lag Theory

When applied to Appalachia, cultural lag theory depicts a traditionalist subculture unable to adapt to the modern world (Photiadis, n.d.; Photiadis, 1970). Weller (1965) views indigenous Appalachians as representatives of a folk culture and looks to the lives of the early mountaineers to find the sources of present-day living patterns. In Weller's view, the virtues of the early mountaineers, their rugged independence and fearlessness, have been transformed by a changing environment into behavioral characteristics that set them apart from middle-class Americans and account for their continued poverty. Traits attributed to Appalachians are selfish individualism, traditionalist values, fatalism, orientation to action and impulsivity, stoicism and introversion, and orientation to persons rather than objects. Weller also contrasts the sharp role distinctions between genders in Appalachia with the supposedly more equitable gender relationships in middle-class America.

Stephenson (1968) sums up the effect this postulated cultural lag has had on the children of low-status Appalachians.

> The traditional mountain culture has been likened to a 'frontier culture,' in that it is adapted to a stationary condition it is not geared for change or for adaptation to new conditions. Therefore the persons who are socialized into it are not prepared for change either, and they lack the kinds of cultural tools--the thoughtways, habits of looking ahead, the constant circumspection and vigilance for changes in the very conditions of existence--which are the keys to survival in middle-class, industrial society. . . . They have little talent for scanning all possible alternative solutions to a problem and rationally selecting the one best suited for a long range, optimal outcome. (p. 192)

Personality Trait Theory

Belief in the significance of early childhood influences on the formation of the characteristics of low-status adults has led to a search for the causes of poverty in socialization patterns. This has resulted in a conception of change-resistant adult personalities and has put an exaggerated emphasis on intergenerational poverty (Allen, 1970). The developmental theory that informs this model of Appalachian poverty appears to be grounded in ego psychology, although this is often more implicit than explicit. This psychological bias is implied in descriptions of the Appalachian subculture that picture the mountaineer frustrated by a world that devalues him, turning his anger inward and becoming apathetic (Ball, 1968; Photiadis, n.d.). In this view the injured ego compensates by developing dysfunctional defenses. The view is then reified in evaluations that assign psychiatric diagnoses to what are identified as regional character traits (Looff 1971; Polansky et al., 1972).

Parenting in Culture-of-Poverty Theory

The assumption that specific parenting patterns are instrumental in forming adults who are inadequate in their basic psychological makeup is apparent in research that has focused on Appalachian family organization and interaction (Looff, 1971; Polansky et al., 1972). Living in sparsely settled areas, early mountain inhabitants had to depend on the available resources of the nuclear family. Over time, intermarriage between kin groups enlarged this resource network. Loyalty to the kinship group held a high survival value in a society of subsistence farmers. The gradual modernization of Appalachia has produced changes in this way of life, but kinship groups still reside in close proximity and maintain strong emotional ties.

Weller (1965) defines Appalachian families as adult centered in contrast to the child-centered families of the middle class. In an adult-centered family, children are accorded little special identity, except when indulged as infants, and home life is structured around adult needs. Discipline is described as lax, most often only threatened and likely to be delivered when child behavior infringes on adult prerogatives.

Two prominent studies, conducted in the early 1970s, touch on the socialization process in low-income or low-status rural Appalachian families. Although these studies are concerned with special populations, families with psychologically disturbed children (Looff, 1971) and neglectful mothers (Polansky et al., 1972), their conclusions have influenced present-day images of low-status women.

Looff, generalizing from his experience in rural mental health practice, maintains that the most common mental health problems in rural Appalachia are school-phobia, dependent and hysterical personality disorders, conversion reactions, and elective mutism. Women, viewed in their maternal role, are described as so nurturing, warm, and indulgent (a personality strength) that they become over-protective, potentially pathogenically so. Another negative result of this strong orientation to feelings is said to be a lack of control of aggressive impulses.

In addressing the special problems of the very poor, Looff does warn against generalizations regarding poverty populations, pointing to the diversity of experience in differing environments. He also recognizes the role of insufficient economic opportunities and resources in creating stresses that are interactive with individual personality configurations.

Social workers (Chilman, 1968; Polansky et al., 1972) have used the culture-of-poverty model in their analyses of low-status parents. The long-term reliance in social work education on the psychoanalytic or ego psychology model of development as a primary knowledge base has created an affinity with the tacit assumptions of the psychological trait perspective in the culture-of-poverty model.

Critiques of Poverty Theories as Applied to Appalachians

Both cultural-lag theories and attributions of pathological personality characteristics to low-status Appalachians have been challenged. Billings (1974) has contested the concept of Appalachia as a region with a distinct subculture. His analysis of attitude items in a 1965 North Carolina survey of low-income families and individuals found that the weakest predictor of middle-class orientation was region, coming after education, age, urban-rural differences, blue collar-white collar differences, and race. Fisher (1976) contends that subcultural models have been developed by writers already committed to that view and have been descriptive in nature. Lewis (1978) has pointed out that the by-product of such descriptive approaches has been the identification of elements of the subculture as causal agents in perpetuating poverty while ignoring or minimizing the effect of changes in the social, economic, and political environment. A similar descriptive method has been used in the labeling of personality characteristics seen in low-status individuals. The validity of characteristics attributed to persons of low status was questioned by Allen (1970) who reviewed the research relating personality and poverty. He concluded that "most of the demonstrated relationships between personality and poverty are quite weak" (p. 259).

Theoretically the culture-of-poverty model is problematic because it fails to examine the interaction of larger societal forces and the situational quality of life in low-status groups. It also ignores the coping strength and adaptive value of behaviors developed in response to the reality of an inequitable society.

Situational Theories of Poverty

The impact of economic exploitation and cultural imperialism on the welfare of Appalachian communities and families has been assessed by Gaventa (1980) and Lewis and Knipe (1978). These observers locate the economic problems of the Appalachian region in the usurping of the area's resources by outside moneyed interests and depict women and men who are powerless to control the profits of their labor.

The dominant situational explanation of Appalachian poverty is based on internal colonialist theory. Writers using the colonialist model take a political perspective toward Appalachian history and contend that one cannot isolate a culture from its larger societal context. Lewis, Kobak, and Johnson (1978) and Whisnant (1980) view the contemporary family system as an adaptation to the conditions created by the capitalist exploitation of the region's resources, such as coal and timber.

Beginning in the latter part of the nineteenth century, Appalachian land was bought cheaply and tenant farmers were forced from their homes. Wages paid to workers in the mines and later the textile factories were so low that the workers lived lives of servitude to the company. Attempts to unionize the industries of Appalachia prior to World War II led to bloodshed and oppression.

The already strong family system became the refuge for the embattled mountaineers. The family supplied the emotional warmth and economic backup needed by the native workers facing the dangers of the company coal mines and the impersonality of factory life. The family became by necessity the protector of the clan's cultural history and traditional ways, a bulwark against assimilation into hostile or strange environments. It is this turning inward of the family that is said to have produced patterns of parenting that have been labeled overprotective.

From the perspective of the internal colonialist conceptualization, women are accorded a more heroic role than is acknowledged by other outlooks. Women are charged with caring for the home and children, but they also have been active in supporting their menfolk in the struggle to obtain decent living conditions (Kahn, 1972). Depictions of Appalachians as silent types, suspicious of strangers, are reinterpreted in this perspective as realistic conduct for people defending their families.

Two of the significant differences between the culture-of-poverty and internal colonialist perspectives lie in their reconstruction of the origins of observed family patterns and their conclusions regarding the significance of these patterns in the lives of individual low-status Appalachians. Some common ground exists in their observations. All would agree that blood kinship is one of the most important elements in the Appalachian family, and although there may be conflicts within the extended family, the family will nevertheless present a united front to the outside world.

Adherents of the colonialism model do not deny that some low-status individuals are poorly prepared to compete in the cultural mainstream, but they contend that factors in the larger social context have contributed to the creation of this problem. Billings (1974) points to the need for increased understanding of how the situational variables in the economic, political, and social sphere interact with the life processes of low-status people.

Social Stratification in Appalachia

Some ethnographic studies in Appalachia report a clear stratification process with some variation of high, middle, and low strata (Keefe, Reck, & Reck, 1985; Schwarzweller et al., 1971; Stephenson, 1968). A common assumption is that the critical demarcation between social strata is determined by each group's level of adaptation to the norms and life styles of the urban middle class. Low-status groups are seen as least assimilated to the new norms, and women in this category are said to be bound by traditional sex-role mores (Gochros, 1974; Kaplan, 1971; Photiadis, 1970). Traditional female role behavior, restrictions in the choice of role models, and limited employment opportunities are all seen as factors affecting the occupational aspirations of women (Photiadis, 1986). Schwarzweller et al. (1971) and Beaver (1976) report that egalitarianism is an important principle in traditional Appalachian society, but they both demonstrate that this ideal coexists with a stratification system and the resulting incongruity is rationalized.

Working in a small community of 52 families, Beaver (1976) found that an ideology of egalitarianism was the basis for social interaction. But the residents did perceive two distinct social groups: "most folks around here" and "worthless folks." Beaver defines *worth* as an inherent quality attributed to all until proven otherwise. People are considered worthless when they are too lazy to work, although they are physically able, and have become dependent on social service agencies. Some deviant behaviors, such as alcoholism, illegitimate pregnancy, or criminal activity, may render a person worthless, but individual circumstances are considered within a given community context.

Schwarzweller et al. (1971) gathered data in a comparable community of 77 Appalachian families in 1942 with a follow up in 1961. They encountered the concept of worth/worthlessness but found it was bound to a clear stratification system founded on economic achievement and behavioral norms.

Perceptions of stratification differentials become part of the life view transmitted to children in different social groups through the socialization process. This principle is operative in Appalachian society. Despite an outward show of egalitarianism, everyone in a given rural community knows which families are worthless, and this label becomes part of family members' identity whether they are dealing with the neighborhood grocer, the school principal, or the welfare worker.

Low-Status Appalachian Women

Histories or documentations of contemporary life add first-hand accounts of the ordinary lives of individual women to the record (Kahn, 1972; Lewis, Selfridge, et al., 1986). Women in this type of study are portrayed as proud and decent with a natural dignity. The realities of their uncompromising environment and the economic exploitation of their families may have led to feelings of frustration and anger but have also motivated efforts to resist future exploitation (Kahn, 1972). The women are noted as showing "courage, humor and strength in the face of formidable odds" (Smith, 1986:4).

It is in the nature of this type of literature to feature the positive characterological aspects of the subjects. But such writing also demonstrates that a central feature of these women's lives is their role as the protector of the emotional well-being of the family, whether nuclear or single-parent. These women have been called upon to comfort and cater to men who have faced failure and humiliation. They must attempt to defend their children against the slurs and prejudices of those who have superior economic positions. They have banded together to protest the industrial insults to their families and their environment. But the documents also make it clear that this role expectation--to be a strong, emotionally supportive woman--has a price: fatigue, emotional depletion, depression, and frustrated anger that can result in periodic emotional dysfunction.

The perspectives of low-status women discussed up to this point may seem, at times, contradictory. Are they unsophisticated hedonists, apathetic drudges, or stoic protectors of the family? The wide variety of reported perceptions are probably attributable to the range of persons and behaviors encountered by the observers, the range of observers with their various levels of observational interests dictated by different professional disciplines, and the underlying ideological positions that structure the studies. It is certainly feasible that much of what has been reported is true for some part of the population under discussion at some time.

But there is a further dimension that can be added to enhance an understanding of the social world of low-status women in Appalachia. This dimension can be derived from an analysis of the ways the women describe and explain themselves. For the women under discussion are more than products of their social context or the sum of their psychological characteristics: they are also active creators of their own reality.

CHAPTER THREE

RESEARCH METHODS

This study was designed to honor the integrity of each participant's world view through the use of qualitative methods for data collection, including unstructured, open-ended interviews and participant observation. The investigator took up part-time residence with a family in the participant's community. This provided the opportunity for an ethnographic perspective, the chance to observe the women in their social context. The methods used to gather the data are consistent with the theoretical base of the study and are derived from symbolic interactionist research and ethnography. Grounded theory methodology was used to process the data and to discover the social processes revealed by the participants.

The Chicago School of symbolic interactionists, exemplified by H.G. Blumer, maintains that social interaction is a formative process, not simply a medium wherein determining factors produce behavior. Individuals use the available cultural set of meanings to fashion their own interpretation of events in their social world. In conducting research, symbolic interactionists have used a variety of qualitative data sources, including life histories, autobiographies, case studies, diaries, letters, non-directive interviews, and participant observation. They avoid the predetermination of variables to be studied on the grounds that such an approach renders the world in mechanistic terms (Meltzer, Petras & Reynolds, 1967).

This perspective is also present in the field of anthropology as researchers have applied the ethnographic method to the study of groups within their own cultures. Ethnography is a holistic research method aimed at "the more general process of understanding another human group" (Agar, 1980:71). Unlike the linear progression of the hypothetico-deductive methodologist who proceeds from hypothesis to data collection to analysis, the ethnographer goes directly into the social situation of interest and by observing and talking with people attempts to discover embedded categories of meaning. The ethnographic method is an attempt to understand what Imre (1982) means by implicit knowledge, knowledge that is contextual. This method is concerned with the beliefs and values that are woven into the fabric of the common-sense world and that are used to define meaning in a personal context (Agar, 1980; Agar, 1986; Pelto, & Pelto, 1978; Spradley, 1980).

Grounded theory refers to a research process based on the use of inductive reasoning. Empirical data, consisting of the researcher's observations and the participants' statements, are used to generate conceptual categories and define their properties. The data are then analyzed for patterns of relationships occurring between categories as a means of elucidating the concepts and developing an explanatory theory that fits the data. Proponents of grounded theory claim that it can provide accurate evidence because it uses natural observations, enables the investigator to develop empirical generalizations, assists in specifying concepts worthy of in-depth study, and makes possible the generation and verification of theory (Chenitz & Swanson, 1986; Glaser, 1978; Glaser & Strauss, 1967; Mullen, 1986; Turner, 1981, 1983).

Study Site

The study was conducted in Cocke County, Tennessee, a rural East Tennessee county in Appalachia. It was chosen as the site for the study because the author was familiar with the community and because its population is largely rural (75% of the population live outside of its two small towns) and native born (87% are native Tennesseans). The county maintains a stable population of about 29,000, 8000 of whom reside in the county seat, Newport. Forty-seven percent of the population claim to be of English, Irish and German descent. The small minority population, 2% African-American and 0.7% Spanish-American, largely reside in Newport (US Census, 1980).

The news media have portrayed Cocke County as epitomizing traditional mountain culture. Dating from the years when Cocke County supplied moonshine whiskey to surrounding dry, urban areas, the county developed a reputation for violence and illegal activity, "hillbilly" style

(Anson, 1981). This reputation has continued to the present with media focussing attention on clandestine cock fights, marijuana growers battling the government helicopters that patrol their skies, and "chop shops" where stolen cars are stripped so parts can be resold (Smith, 1985).

Situated at the conflux of three rivers, the Pigeon, the Nolichucky, and the French Broad, Cocke County's arable valleys rise from 1400 to over 6600 feet in the Great Smoky Mountains. It was settled in 1783 and became a political entity as early as 1797. The first settlers had to battle Indians to carve out their farms and establish the small village of Newport. Poor roads kept the community relatively isolated until the railroad opened the region, arriving in Newport in 1867. In the 1880s the lumber industry began to develop and joined agriculture as part of the economic base of the community. Subsistence farming was the basis for family self-sufficiency.

After World War I, inhabitants began more and more to grow cash crops such as tobacco and vegetables that were sold to nearby canning factories (Godshalk, 1970). Families then became increasingly dependent on wages and agricultural price fluctuations. For many this spelled the end of their self-sufficient life style.

By the 1950s and 1960s Cocke County began to attract small businesses and industries, that were enticed by non-union cheap labor. But during the recessions of the 1970s many of these employers left the area (Maples, 1968). The promotion of tourism and its associated businesses is now a major economic strategy.

Unemployment is high, averaging over 20% in the winter months. Only 40% of the adult residents have graduated from high school. The tourist industry in near by areas, such as Gatlinburg and Pigeon Forge, provides temporary summer employment, usually consisting of minimum wage jobs in service occupations for women. Residents must have reliable transportation to take advantage of such job opportunities.

Almost one quarter (23.68%) of the families in the county have incomes below the poverty level (U.S. Census, 1980) and are receiving food stamps (Tennessee Advisory Commission on Intergovernmental Relations, 1985). Cocke County has the highest rate of low-birth-weight infants in the region and an infant mortality rate of 16.3% (Tennessee Health Improvement Council, 1984-1985). As the foregoing statistics attest, many people in Cocke County have no access to the prosperity enjoyed by middle America.

Selection of Participants

The researcher sought as participants women who were rural Appalachian-born and raised (preferably in Cocke County), currently raising children in their homes, living below the rural poverty standard, and deemed by the referrer as average or not unusual for their social group. Referrals of appropriate participants were solicited from professionals in the community who had regular contact with low-status mothers and children such as the staff of the Public Health-sponsored Child Development Program; East Tennessee Human Resources Agency, Homemaker Services; and the Douglas Cherokee Community Action Program. Twelve of the 14 households that participated in the study were referred by staff at the Child Development Program.

Several possible categories of local women were either deliberately excluded from the study or were unavailable for participation. In the first category were women experiencing, severe family or legal problems. It was the researcher's belief that participation in a research study might increase the already high stress levels in the lives of these women. A number of the study participants, however, had experienced periods of serious family problems in the past.

Also excluded from the study were local African-American women. The researcher made this decision after interviewing a young mother referred by an African-American professional in the community. There are about 670 African-American residents in Cocke County, comprising 200 households. This small ethnic community has always been surrounded by considerable prejudice and discrimination. There are still parts of this county whose residents boast of their "sundown law," that is, no African-Americans allowed there after dark.

The African-American mother who was interviewed felt that she had experienced prejudice in her dealings with local whites. She had been socialized within a small ethnic enclave, and all of her social contacts were within that group. She had more education than the white participants, having attended college for two years. African-American women in this community appeared to the researcher to have a different social reality than the study participants and so were not included in the study. A study of the social reality of rural, African-American Appalachian women could reveal in what ways this respondent's perceptions were typical of her social group.

Research Methods

Two categories of women were unavailable to the researcher. In the first group were women whose social contacts are completely controlled by their husbands. Local health professionals spoke of such women but said the husbands barely tolerated their interactions with the women and thus the professionals were reluctant to refer the women to the researcher. Several participants in this study (see particularly references to Lorraine and Reena) indicated that at some point in their marriages their husbands had controlled all aspects of their lives. The perceptions of these women may be relevant to the lives of the women who were thus excluded from the study.

Also unavailable were women from the low-status group who had either married non-local men and left the area, who had married local men and migrated to urban areas, or who had found other means to leave the county. The researcher did hear stories about women who had left the area and achieved a higher economic standard of living than their local relatives. The informants said that such women did not often visit local kin.

The researcher first attempted to visit the homes of the women who had been referred to discuss their consent to participate in the study. Once in the home on subsequent visits, she added other adult women in the home to the study, with their consent. She was not able to contact all of the women referred due to difficulties in communicating with referrals who did not have telephones or were frequently away from home. The researcher arbitrarily stopped accepting referrals after the 14 households agreed to participate in the study and when it became clear there would be insufficient time to follow up on further referrals.

Participant Characteristics

In Appalachia, as in the rest of the United States, female-headed households are over-represented in poverty groups. In the Southern Appalachian region, which includes all of Tennessee's Appalachian counties, 11% of the male-headed families with children live in poverty compared to 36.8% of the female-headed families (Tickamyer, & Tickamyer, 1986).

All the households in this research have incomes below the rural poverty level. Nuclear family groups are, however, more likely to have some earned income than female-headed households. The majority of the families existed on some combination of Aid to Dependent Children,

Social Security, or VA benefits, supplemented by food stamps. Few of the women have ever worked outside the home.

The 18 participants, all mothers, range in age from 21 to 67, although more than half of them are in their twenties. They represented 14 different households. Three households contain nuclear families, parents and children. Nine households include extended family members. Six of these homes are female headed and three consist of parents, children, and other family members, often a grandparent. Two other households are female-headed, containing only a mother and her children. This is representative of the varied family compositions so seldom noted in Appalachian studies. Five women are married, six are divorced, two separated, two widowed, and three have never married.

This group of women have a fertility rate considerably higher than the national rate of fewer than two pregnancies per woman. The women under thirty have averaged three pregnancies apiece and the middle group have an average of 6.6 pregnancies. One participant in her sixties had 20 pregnancies--more than double the pregnancies of anyone else in the group. Although the women under thirty had stayed in school a few years longer than the older women, only one has graduated from high school and one has a GED.

Data Analysis

Data for this study include observations made on site in the form of field notes made during the five months the researcher was in residence in the county. These notes were dictated into a tape recorder immediately following the interactions in the field, and an expanded version was typed within a week of the contact. The researcher also kept a personal journal.

The analysis of the field notes was an ongoing process starting shortly after taking up residence in Cocke County. The constant comparative method was used to begin analysis of the field notes. Data were compared, paragraph by paragraph, for similarities and differences. As this was done, the data were coded on a series of cards containing descriptive labels or terms derived from the data. For example, an early card contains maternal caretaking activities, whereas later cards contain data on perceived consequences of rural residency and feeling "put down."

The initial coding process generated over sixty codes containing notations of the linkages between cards, that is, cards that appear to be connected conceptually or that touched on aspects of the same subject. Gradually these cards were sorted and grouped into larger conceptual categories. During the course of this process, other topic areas to be explored appeared and were included in the ongoing data collection. This is referred to as theoretical sampling, in that the ongoing data analysis suggests further sources of information. This might mean interviewing participants from additional sites, adding specific types of participants to the study, or adding a specific area of questions to future interviews (Chenitz & Swanson, 1986; Mullen, 1986). Toward the end of the study, for example, the concept of boundaries, both geographic and psychological, emerged in the data and later interviews reflect direct questioning of participants about this concept as well as discussions of this subject with local women from different socioeconomic groups.

Writing started almost immediately. This took the form of memos in which the researcher began to define conceptual categories using the data on specific cards, noting ideas and connections between concepts stimulated through the analysis process, and exploring theoretical connections between categories. Memo writing was a cumulative process, in which later memos built on, integrated, and expanded the thinking of earlier memos. Through memo writing, the core concepts and hypotheses began to emerge from the data. It was at this point that the researcher began to explore the linkages between her findings and already existing theory.

Ideally, grounded theory research should reveal underlying social processes or basic patterns in social life. These might be either social psychological processes drawn from individual behavior or social structural processes found in organizational behaviors (Mullen, 1986).

Research Validity

Questions of validity and reliability are as important in qualitative research as they have been in quantitative work. They cannot be approached in equivalent terms, however, due to the nature of qualitative studies, in which the instrument is the observer and the measurements are cultural observations translated into categories and themes. Validity is achieved in qualitative studies by providing for different and multiple exposures to the problem of interest, checking the researcher's observations and the validity of original data through contacts with a variety of people in multiple situations, and by framing questions meant to confirm or contradict working hypotheses. As Kirk and Miller (1986) point out:

> To the extent that confirmatory methods are used, they are used quickly and informally, rather than constituting entire research projects in and of themselves, and they belong to the data-collection rather than the analysis phase of research. (p. 31)

In the course of this study, the researcher's residence in the community provided many opportunities to seek information from a variety of sources, including her landlady and the director of the local welfare office. Personnel in the local health care system were particularly helpful as sounding boards and informants as the researcher began to air her emerging thoughts about the social processes she was observing.

Research Reliability

Reliability is a difficult issue in qualitative studies because the research process is difficult to replicate. Some forms of reliability testing are patently inappropriate in ethnographic work. One cannot expect a single method of observation, for example, to yield significant data about a complex social situation, nor for any measurement of the spontaneous world to remain unchanged through time as in test/retest procedures. Neither can any set of measurements or observations hope to capture more than a small part of the rich social context under study. With that understanding, the researcher has used the following procedures to clarify her research process:

1. Spelled out her theoretical biases both in her proposal and in this dissertation.

2. Delineated her analytic process.

3. Retained field notes and documents developed during analysis.

4. Checked the hypotheses drawn from the data with people representative of different status groups in the community.

Limitations of the Study

One of the limitations of this study is that the women who participated cannot be proven to be a representative sample of low-status Appalachian women and the wider applicability of the cultural themes of their lives might be questioned. As has been noted, this study was limited to Caucasian women. Women living with men who severely limit their communications with outsiders and low-status women who have left the community were not available for study. The degree to which the low-income mothers of Cocke County are representative of other Appalachian mothers might also be questioned. It will require further research to ascertain if the findings of this study are applicable in different types of Appalachian communities.

Because of the researcher's years of association with low-status mothers in this area of Appalachia, she did not come to this study with the freshness of perspective that many ethnographers possess when they first enter new cultural groups. Valuable first impressions were, of necessity, missing. Her familiarity with the setting did aid her in establishing rapport in the community, but it left the possibility that previously formed opinions and theories about this cultural world could intrude into her findings. One of the strengths of the grounded theory method is that it forces the researcher to stay close to her data and eschew theories that cannot be supported by the data. This was effective in helping the researcher suspend her prejudgments during the course of this research.

CHAPTER FOUR

FAMILY ROLES AND EXPECTATIONS

The findings of this study support descriptions of low-status Appalachian women to be found in the available literature that discusses the dominance of traditional family values and the personalization of interactions. Traditionalist women have been described as women who accept motherhood as the core of their identity. Marriage and home are the sources of their security, and they retain close connections within their kinship networks (Bernard, 1981).

The women in this study believe that a woman's primary role is to bear children and raise and protect them. Most of these women want to live in a nuclear family with the male provider present. They accept sharply differentiated sex roles and are comfortable when men and women have different social spheres. In addition to their traditionalist stance regarding family and gender roles, the women enter social transactions with expectations that they will be treated fairly and equitably with attention to their individuality. When the women do not receive equitable and personalized responses from others in their social environment, some of them silently withdraw from the situation while others express anger or dissatisfaction.

This study reveals that far from feeling defeated by the rejection they experience in social interactions--particularly with higher-status individuals--the women have intense feelings about negative encounters. They hold firmly to their beliefs about the egalitarian basis of social behavior while labeling the offending other person as rude or socially inadequate. Furthermore, such negative encounters with others do not appear to permanently affect the women's self-appraisals, which are buttressed by their adherence to traditional values and their role performances as mothers.

Female Roles

The women's expectations for female behavior in the context of the family are dominated by an emphasis on the care and protection of children. In all three of their important life roles: mother, daughter, and wife, the women expect to meet the needs and wishes of parents, husbands, and children. Even the small pleasure some of the women may find in becoming working girls is subject to cancellation by their family. Being a mother is the central concern of their lives and the endless return of adult children and the assumption of care for grandchildren ensures that mothering remains an active, life long occupation and status.

Motherhood

Motherhood is the major social role anticipated by the women. For some women the desire to be a mother "when I grow up" was clearly identified by early adolescence. When asked to remember what they wanted from life when they were age 13 or 14, these women spoke of their desire to be mothers and to have large families. "I wanted to be a mother just like my mother and to have 14 children like she did." "Since I was an only child raised by my grandmother, I wanted to have the big family I'd missed."

There were exceptions to these early expectations of self as a mother, but alternative roles were not attained. Some women had girlhood desires to become a nurse, and a few hoped to have some other type of paid employment. But only one of the women had taken any steps during her educational years to achieve an occupational goal. Norene had joined the Job Corps to pursue a career in nursing, but she came home after only one week. She became so anxious away from home, living with strangers, that she became ill. Within a year of coming home she was married.

The strength of the family in determining the women's role choices seems unlimited. Several women had fantasized working outside the home. Ida identified with her older sisters and wanted to go to work with them in the textile mills when she quit school at age 12. But the family thought she should remain at home. She was married when she was 15 and never sought outside employment. Seventeen-year-old Caren wants to move to town when she turns 18 and get a job. Her family says "no way."

Planning pregnancies. As a group, the women in the study have exercised little control over their reproductive lives. The women over thirty began child bearing immediately following marriage, rarely use birth control, and have had repeated pregnancies with little or no attempt to space their children. Cora had six pregnancies in six years with only four live births. This was so detrimental to her reproductive system that a total hysterectomy was necessary. After five pregnancies, Lorraine was having "female trouble." She reluctantly took birth control pills for less than a year but was fearful that the pill could cause cancer. After her sixth pregnancy, a hysterectomy was recommended. The younger women seem to have begun their families in much the same pattern but show an inclination to limit the number of children after three or four pregnancies. This is most often accomplished by a tubal ligation.

Family planning is not ignored, but situational factors frequently interrupt such planning. Barbara is married and has four children under the age of five. She takes birth control pills but is not always able to attend the Public Health clinic to obtain refills. She cannot get enough child car seats in her auto to make the trip to the clinic and has to wait until a friend or family member can sit with the children. She attempted to arrange a tubal after her last delivery, but her Medicaid was cut off (in error) before the baby came. If she becomes pregnant again she would not even consider abortion.

The reasons given for termination of reproductive activity are economic. Because the women's concern is to provide for the children they do have, they continue to see themselves as good mothers in that respect.

Some observers of Appalachia (Polansky, et al., 1972; Weller, 1965) have cited low-status women's reproductive behavior as an example of their impulsivity or present-oriented nature. Such an interpretation implies that conception is a by-product of unrestrained or hedonistic sexual activity. This type of labeling seems unwarranted in light of the women's strong orientation toward motherhood. Their implicit expectation is that they will become mothers sooner or later.

When is not important. Methods for spacing pregnancies are not plentiful. Some methods, such as abortion, are morally unacceptable to the women; others, such as birth control pills, are not always obtainable due to transportation and child-care problems. None of the women held their partner responsible for preventing conception. Medicaid payment for tubal ligations has provided an acceptable means of limiting family size.

Being a good mother. All of the study participants perceive their activities as mothers as central to their lives, constituting their major social role. Thus the requirements of this role present the longest and most articulated family role description in the study. The women talk about the positive and negative qualities of the women who mothered them, complain about women they knew who were not good mothers, enumerate and demonstrate their own accomplishments as mothers, and speak of the exhausting task of raising a family on a limited income.

The following characteristics of the good mother emerged from their varied stories. A good mother is happy to have children, is unselfish, and always puts the children's needs before her own. She ensures that the children's basic needs for food, shelter, and clothing are met and protects them from physical harm. She accepts her children and grandchildren unconditionally and tries to be a good role model for her daughters.

The importance of children is testified to by the women who report having chosen their children's welfare over and above their relationships with a male partner, whether or not he was the children's father. Lorraine finally evicted her alcoholic husband after he struck their daughter. Marilyn said she divorced the children's step father after she found bruises on her baby. Reena left her husband after years of abuse when she had to choose between staying and possibly losing custody of her children. She explained, "My children are everything to me." Nancy said she doubted that she would ever marry because she didn't believe she could find a man who would "treat these two young ones (her two children born out of wedlock) right."

Being an unselfish mother. A good mother welcomes all of her pregnancies and does not attempt to terminate any of them. She is saddened if she miscarries and always counts both the miscarried infants and children who died after birth when recounting her reproductive status. Norene even keeps track of how old the twins that she miscarried would be if they had survived. A good mother does not consider abortion a reproductive option even when her pregnancy is the result of rape.

She does not desert her children, live with a man who mistreats her children, nor seek her own happiness at her children's expense. They are considered a life long obligation. Activities for the mother's benefit may be postponed to meet the child's needs. Eunice, a grandmother in her fifties, needed to go to Knoxville for a cardiac evaluation. Her pregnant daughter, Doris, said, "Now Mamma, you know you can't go away until this baby is born." And indeed, Eunice has not gone for her tests and is providing child care for the new infant.

A good mother ensures her children's basic needs are met. She first looks to her husband, if married, to provide the economic resources in the family. If this fails, she will locate all the local resources for assistance and even beg if need be. If she has never lived with the children's father, she will assume total responsibility for the children from birth. All aspects of child care fall to her. Her children remain with her at all times. They go where she goes.

Mothers are the family emissaries to all social agencies. Although a father may drive the mother to an agency, he will wait in the car while she transacts all the family business. She will keep numerous appointments to obtain or retain services, and will even venture to large metropolitan areas, which are frightening even to consider, to obtain the special services her children require.

Keeping them from harm. A good mother protects her children. It is her responsibility to keep her children from harm. Specifically, she does not allow anyone to tease them and hurt their feelings, to do them bodily harm, or to abuse them sexually. Cora says that one of the reasons she won't leave her shack in the hills for the housing projects in town is her fear that her grandchildren will be teased or blamed for trespassing in neighbor's yards. When one of her daughter's adolescent male friends teased one of the grandchildren and made him cry, Cora became so angry she threw what she had in her hand at him. It was an open can of tomato sauce.

The good mother is expected particularly to guard her daughters from sexual molestation or voluntary sexual activity that results in pregnancy without marriage. The emphasis on the protection of female children may be due to the gender of the informants. But it is also a part of the development of strong bonds between mothers and daughters that leads them to live their lives in close proximity to one another. Within this injunction to protect one's daughters there exists a hierarchy of behaviors. First and most important is to protect the daughter from sexual molestation by male family members, then to protect her from men outside the family, and lastly, to protect her from herself, that is, teach her to avoid voluntary sexual activity outside of marriage. A mother's failure to protect her daughter from male family members may result in complete estrangement between mother and daughter. Judy not only will have nothing to do with her mother, but has incurred her mother's anger for gaining custody of her younger siblings. When Judy was in her mid-teens, her mother didn't believe her claim that her stepfather attempted to fondle her. Judy left home never to return.

Daughters who have been raped by outsiders do not believe their mothers have failed them. But mothers do try to guard against this. As long as the daughter continues to reside at home, the mother believes she bears some responsibility for the younger woman's sexual deportment. Eunice made a point of saying that her daughter had not become pregnant outside of marriage until after the daughter had moved away from Eunice's home.

Coming home to Mamma. Adult children come back home periodically to live and may stay indefinitely. A good mother accepts her children and grandchildren unconditionally. This does not mean that the mother may not be critical of a child's behavior, particularly an adult child. But these criticisms do not result in permanent estrangements. A grandmother reported, with disapproval, that the physically handicapped grandchild she is raising is severely impaired due, in part, to her daughter's use of drugs during pregnancy. Yet this daughter received a warm welcome when she showed up after an absence of many months. Another participant was quite critical of one of her daughters and attempted to deter her from having a tubal ligation. But the grandmother provided child care when the daughter proceeded with the disapproved operation.

As part of her acceptance of each child, the good mother does not play favorites. Family resources are to be meted out fairly; every child gets its share. The mother must also not appear to love or pamper one child more than another. When Barbara talks about why she doesn't feel close to her mother, although she visits her daily, she notes that she believes her mother has favored the youngest and oldest children, her two brothers, over herself. Residual feelings of sibling rivalry are evident in stories told by some of the women. Sometimes the mother is faulted as continuing to play favorites among her adult children. Other women seem to be vying for their mother's approval or attention. The importance of mother's acceptance remains strong in these families, for life.

Active motherhood is a life time role for the women in this group. For those over thirty-five the rearing of children has not ceased, although their children have matured, because they have accepted responsibility for raising various grandchildren and even great-grandchildren. In addition, adult children and other relatives may move in and out of their home when they are in economic trouble. During the five months covered by this study, Lorraine shared her home with her unmarried daughter and the two grandchildren she was raising. But when another daughter, son-in-law, and three grandchildren moved back from Alabama, she moved them in for a few months until they could get jobs and find a cheap place to rent. Cora was raising four grandchildren and her teenage daughter, but also provided housing over a period of four months for another teenage daughter who had just had a baby, the girl's new husband, Cora's two young-adult daughters, and the male friend of one of these daughters. Women in this group do not seem to confront the role changes that are referred to as the empty nest syndrome. One of the benefits of the maternal role in this group seems to be the feeling that one is always needed.

The expectation of nurturing behavior is not limited to one's procreative family, but is thought equally desirable in one's family of origin. The women gave numerous examples of arranging their own lives in order to care for a family member. Nancy quit school to help her mother care for a disabled sibling. Judy is rearing her younger siblings who were in need of protective care. Kitty feels guilty because she was unable to nurse her terminally ill grandmother due to her responsibilities to husband and children.

Being a role model. A good mother is a proper role model for her daughters. She maintains her self-respect. This expectation is held by adult daughters who, upon reflection, speak of what their mothers "should have done." This standard pertains largely to the mother's relationships with men. She is expected to stand up for herself and protect herself from physical abuse even if it means leaving her male partner.

This expectation has been a source of conflict for some of the participants and may be superseded by their expectations for a good wife where "stand-by-your-man" is a major theme. It may also conflict with the mother's beliefs about what she must endure to ensure her children are provided for economically. Nancy said she would never allow a man to treat her the way her father had treated her mother. Nancy now lives with her mother, Nora. Speaking of those beatings, Nora put her head down, and said, "I know I shouldn't have let him do that, but I thought I had to put up with it for you children's sake."

It should be noted that a woman does not have to be married to the father of her child or any other man to be a good mother. Despite the fact that both parents may adopt a highly protective attitude toward their daughters while they reside at home, once an illegitimate pregnancy occurs neither mother nor child are rejected. If the unmarried mother then performs according to the role prescriptions in this group, she may obtain approval according to the women in this study.

Working and mothering. Josie and Barbara have been periodically employed since they married, but only when their husbands are unemployed. They always return home to resume full-time mothering when their men find jobs. Although they have typically held low-paying service jobs, both women enjoy outside employment. But being employed outside the home never takes precedence over the roles of wife and mother. When a wife and/or mother is employed outside the home she accepts her family's prescription for her performance. She is expected to fulfill the role of wife and mother as well as meet the requirements of her employment, to abide by her husband's decisions regarding when and where she will work, to quit her job if any family member decides she is needed at home, and to put her earnings into the family coffers because the justification for her employment is the economic need of the family.

Being a Good Mother's Daughter

The women in this group demonstrate close and enduring relationships between mothers and daughters. Mother-daughter relationships are the most stable family relationships in this group. Five of the women reside with one or more of their adult daughters, and two of these households appear to be long-term arrangements. Several other

Family Roles and Expectations

women live adjacent to their mothers or daughters or they visit them frequently. Only one woman is so estranged from her mother that she has no contact with her.

In contrast, the women did not reveal the same emotional closeness or physical proximity to their fathers. In talking about their early family life, they either omitted their fathers from their narratives or commented on negative paternal behaviors that had affected their lives. Neither did the women appear to have regular interactions with their fathers in the present. Eunice's mother is dead and her elderly father continues to reside in Cocke County. When Eunice's daughter mentioned she had run into Grandpa at the grocery, it was apparent that Eunice had little interest in his condition and had not seen him in some time. This lack of close involvement with the father may be related either to the strict separation of parental roles in these families where the mother is responsible for all child rearing activities, or to the high incidence of absent or abusive fathers in this group.

Mothers also appear to have close bonds with their sons, but adult sons are not as likely to maintain close physical proximity as are daughters. Detailed information on the role of sons was not forthcoming. However, in a few of the families interviewed, the husband has maintained close ties with his mother and in all instances the wife was critical of this son-mother dependence. This behavior would appear to conflict with the wife's expectations that the husband will be the family leader and not look to his mother for instructions.

The daughter role is inferred from the women's self-expectations as daughters and from their observed behaviors. The rules for being a good daughter are fewer than those for a good mother, but it is also a life long role. Deviation from these family rules can produce ongoing conflicts between mothers and children, but the children are not cut off or disowned. A good daughter is loyal and will stay in close contact with her mother and family.

Being loyal. A good daughter should put loyalty to the family above her own needs or desires. She will not tell outsiders anything that might cause serious problems for family members. The obvious areas of family life where this injunction is critical are in cases of physical and sexual abuse because these behaviors will provoke outside intervention in the family. Daughters are also held back from public exposure of abuse by their own psychological feelings of guilt and shame. Young women who tell outsiders about sexual abuse may be held responsible for the break up of the family. Four years ago at the age of 13, Caren told a teacher she was being sexually abused by a member of her extended family. This resulted in the man's going to prison. She now feels her entire family is permanently angry with her and believes she did the wrong thing by telling an outsider. However, her parents have not disowned her and, in fact, they do not want her to leave home to seek employment.

A good daughter will abandon her activities to assist in the home when needed. It was not uncommon twenty years ago for daughters to be expected to quit school to help raise the younger children, keep the house, or work in the fields. Illiteracy among older rural women is related, in part, to the necessity in their youth for all family members to perform farm labor in order for the family to survive. Some like Nora, now 67, never went to school at all. Currently, adolescent daughters are not expected to contribute to the family income.

Today a daughter is more likely to leave school to assist in the care of a family member with a long-term illness. Marilyn left school at 14 because her mother had cancer and she nursed her for the next four years. Nancy left school to help with a disabled older brother, and Dorothy left to assist her mother when her father was dying. This requirement for a good daughter may result in role conflict when the daughter is married and believes she cannot take time away from her own husband and children. Kitty believes her family blames her because she had married and was unable to nurse her granny when she had the stroke that eventually led to her death. Kitty says, "I just have to accept the guilt."

A good daughter does not leave home until she is ready to establish her own family. Until that time she will abide by the restrictions set by her parents. She will stay in close contact with her mother even after she is an adult. This is part of the reciprocity of mother/daughter roles. Mothers always accept their children, and daughters' primary loyalties are to their mothers.

The daughter will not abandon her mother. Nancy is disdainful of her sister in a nearby state who "wants to put Mom in a nursing home." Even though Kitty was not raised by her mentally handicapped mother and believes that the mother indulges Kitty's sister, she makes an effort to take the illiterate woman for her food commodities. She will maintain frequent contacts with her mother even if she does not find this comfortable or pleasant experience. Barbara visits her mother almost every evening, even though she believes her mother favors her brothers, and she dislikes her mother's partisan behavior toward the oldest grandchild.

Daughters believe they are not bound by these rules unless their mothers have fulfilled the good mother requirements. Judy has obtained custody of her younger siblings because her mother was not protecting them from the advances of a step father.

The women in the study paint a picture of the good mother and the good daughter that are in large measure compatible with role prescriptions for family behavior in traditional families throughout contemporary America, particularly in working-class and lower-class families (Schneider & Smith, 1973). The continuation of close bonds between adult daughters and their mothers is viewed as virtually universal in our society and thus is not specific to this rural Appalachian sample (Chodorow, 1978; Cohler & Grunebaum, 1981). The women indicated that they believe women can and should live up to their role ideals.

Male Roles

Fatherhood

In their perceptions of male family roles, the women put more emphasis on the discrepancy between the ideal and actual role performance. The women's reflections on the paternal role include recognition of the influence of their particular social and economic environment on their expectations of male behavior. The increase of female-headed households and the incidence of divorce in this status group has reduced the chances that a low-status woman will experience a relationship with a "good father." In fact, none of the women in this study thought they had both a good father and a good husband. At least a third of the women either never lived with their fathers or lost their fathers to divorce or early death. Given the centrality of the provider role for males in this culture and the difficulty that low-status men experience in obtaining lasting employment in rural Appalachia today, the odds are not in favor of their success as fathers and husbands.

The description of the ideal father role was largely drawn by inference from stories of father behaviors of which the women disapproved, with the attendant implications for behaviors that are held to be desirable. A good father provides for his family economically and refrains from abusive behavior within the family. He is protective without being excessively restrictive. When there are no legal bonds, a good father acknowledges his children, does not abandon them, visits the children, and brings gifts. In considering paternal role behavior, the women drew on both their experiences in their families of origin and their interactions with the fathers of their children. Attempting to secure economic provisions and protecting the family are held to be the most important qualities of a good father.

Making the effort. A good father provides economically for his family to the best of his ability. This does not apply if he does not live in the home. Because the standards for a good wife and mother do not usually include economic activities outside the home, the family's dependence on the father's economic activities is total. The amount of income the father earns is obviously important, but it does not determine whether he is or is not a good father. It is the effort he makes for the family that is paramount.

Men who are unable to find work, are too unskilled to work regularly, or who don't even look for work may still be good fathers if they meet the other expectations. Despite the importance of the work expectation, the tolerance for fathers who do not work but otherwise fulfill their role seems to be based on the very real environmental constraints imposed by high unemployment in the region, a dearth of unskilled jobs, and poor educational resources. Men who earn income but do not share it completely with their family, that is, use the money to drink, gamble, and carouse with women, are bad fathers.

Even a chronically unemployed father may be held in high regard if he refrains from violent and abusive behavior toward all family members. A good father not only does not abuse his children, he does not abuse their mother.

Interacting with children. A good father is protective of his daughters without being excessively restrictive. Daughters believe that a good father should allow his late-adolescent daughters to leave home to find work and live independently, although none of the women in the study who lived in homes with fathers did leave before marriage. Apparently, the fathers believe that good daughters do as they are told and should not leave home until they are safely married.

A good father acknowledges the paternity of his children. To the unmarried women in this study the question of paternity is not a legal issue. It becomes a legal issue, however, if they receive AFDC because the Department of Human Services now requires the mother to sue the father for support. When he denies paternity, the mother, child, and putative father all have to go to Knoxville for blood tests and then the parents appear in court. From the woman's perspective, if the man denies paternity there is nothing she can do about it socially, so she may disdain him or shrug it off, maintaining "he isn't worth bothering about." She may allow him very limited interaction with his child, but it is more likely that she will prevent him from seeing the child at all. Because he is considered such a bad father, the child is better off away from him.

A father who acknowledges paternity also contributes to his child's identity in a community in which individuals are frequently identified by their family of origin. Adult daughters who are unsure of their parentage still speculate about whose child they might be.

A good father displays visible interest in his children even if he does not reside in the home. An absent father who acknowledges his children can be a good father if he visits periodically and brings the children gifts. If the parents have not been married, the mother does not expect more substantial support. A father living in the home is expected to interact with his children. But he need not assume any regular responsibilities for them, and his interactions need not take any specific form.

A good father does not abandon his children. Some fathers leave their families and drop out of sight. Even thought initially he made an investment in family life and provided some resources economically and emotionally, if he returns to the family at a later time, he has forfeited the role of a good father.

The expectations for fathering are complementary to, and supportive of, the more detailed mothering role. In order to meet their expectations for the care and protection of their children, the adult women desire a provider who will support their efforts. Conspicuously absent from their expectations are love or romance. This was particularly apparent when they spoke of how they came to marry.

MALE-FEMALE RELATIONSHIPS

For the women in this group the necessary ingredient for realizing their dream of marriage and family is finding a "good man" who will be kind to them and their children and will be able to provide some economic security for their lives. Some do not stop searching for this ideal mate. Marilyn has married three times in search of this elusive dream. She now believes her first love, the man her step father drove away, would have had those qualities.

Most of the women appear to have married or gone to live with the first man in their lives who wanted to have a continuing relationship. Some did this in an eagerness to have their own home and thus to begin to realize their dreams, or to escape the restrictions they felt in their families of origin. Although she was 19 years old and a high-school graduate, Kitty felt she had to abide by her grandfather's rules and he would not let her go out on dates. A relative brought her future husband to visit and after a courtship via telephone, she slipped off and married him. She realizes now that she did not know her husband very well when they married, but she saw him as her means of escape.

The Good Wife

The wife-husband roles are interwoven and complementary in the same model as parental roles, and the rules for being a good wife also apply to females who have a live-in boyfriend. They demonstrate a pattern in which the male occupies the dominant position and the female the compliant position. A wife is expected to remain loyal no matter what happens. She tries to please her husband. In return she expects her man to provide for the family and make the major family decisions. Furthermore, she expects her man to refrain from violent behavior in the home but may find excuses for him when he errs.

Stand by your man. A good wife is loyal to her husband. She stands by her man. A good wife does this without questioning the man about his activities. She trusts him. Her loyalty to her husband and desire to believe him may bring her into conflicts with her daughter when sexual abuse is alleged. If the man does not live up to her expectations, she does not reveal this to others if she can help it. She may lie about her black eye when she has been abused and will keep up pretenses except with the closest family members. The woman's loyalty to her husband may be mixed with personal feelings of shame, which reinforce the injunction to keep the injuries private.

Even when she can admit that her husband fails to fulfill her expectations, she is reluctant to terminate the relationship. Kitty believes she married a man who is not capable of supporting them and their four children due to his limited skills and his dependency on his mother. But she plans to remain in the marriage and has taken responsibility for finding financial resources for the family. Lorraine felt quite isolated raising her four young children in a shack out in the country, but as long as her husband worked and came home at night she felt she should be grateful she had the home and family she had always desired. Although divorce is not uncommon, it is not the choice of a good wife unless she can justify her decision by a higher ethic: the welfare of her children.

Aim to please. A good wife believes she should attempt to please her husband. She tries to keep the house the way he wants, cook the meals he likes, and keep the children from disturbing him too much. Barbara, who has four children is not much concerned with tidiness in her small trailer during the day, but she always straightens up before her husband arrives home from work and keeps things in order on his day off, since a messy house bothers him.

When her man does not fulfill his role as she expects, the good wife blames herself. She attempts to determine what she is doing wrong, or failing to do, that might be causing his undesirable behavior. Reena persisted in looking for her own faults in the face of her husband's chronic alcoholism and abuse.

A good wife continues to be sexually available to her husband no matter what his behavior. Doris made it through two pregnancies despite the fact that her husband refused to take her for any prenatal care, and she feared he'd be too drunk to take her to the midwife's for her delivery. Ida bore her husband several children during the final five years of their marriage even though she knew he had a mistress. He finally left Ida.

A good wife should be sexually naive. It is desirable that she be a virgin when she begins sexual relations with the man she will marry or has married. She remains sexually faithful in her marriage. She should not be exposed to sexuality outside the family context. Eunice was very upset that her daughter-in-law who worked in a nursing home had to clean up bed clothing where male patients had masturbated. She wanted her son, not her daughter-in-law, to complain to the management.

The Good Husband

A good husband provides economically for the family. Similar to the role description of the good father, the good husband is expected to be the main economic provider for the family. If he allows the wife to work outside the home, for brief time periods, it is only to supplement other resources, and she will be expected to terminate her employment when he finds a job.

When a husband is meeting his economic obligations and is not abusive to the children, the wife will not complain much about his role performance in other areas. Husbands who try and are unable to find work can remain good husbands. If unemployed men drink and become violent, they are not good husbands, but their behavior may be excused by a minority of wives. In part, this is based on an assumption that such behavior may be in reaction to the men's feelings about not being able to fulfill their economic roles. These women recognize the stress men in their status group endure due to unemployment, underemployment, or occupational hardships such as assignments to do dirty or dangerous work.

A good husband takes responsibility for the major decisions regarding where the family will reside and how they will live. Along with his economic role, he determines the family life style. A good husband does not defer in these decisions to other people. He particularly does not allow his mamma to interfere in his family. However, this type of interference may actually be prevalent in this status group because of the primacy of the mother-child bond. Most husbands handle the family money, giving their wives what they think they need for household expenses.

A good husband refrains from violent and abusive behavior in the family. He does not drink to excess because this is seen by many women as the trigger for violent behavior. Women have different opinions about the causes of male violence. Some believe it is related to male frustrations in fulfilling their social roles, others think they learned the behavior from their fathers or even mothers, while others see male violence as an expression of their belief in male superiority.

Family Roles and Expectations

A good husband is sexually faithful. Although women expect fidelity, they each have their own tolerance level beyond which this may become an important issue. They usually do not break up their family solely because of male infidelity.

A good husband does not have to help with any household chores or child care. When he does lend a hand at home, it is appreciated but not expected on a regular basis.

Other Family Roles

The only other kin, excluding their children and grandchildren, with whom the women seem to have frequent contact are their siblings. The women provided little information regarding sibling roles. These women do not appear to have close emotional relationships with siblings of either gender. Rivalry for mother's affection and attention is still a major theme in their adult lives. None of the women spoke about having a close emotional tie to any sibling, except for Nancy who still mourns a deceased brother. The elasticity of kinship ties in this group did not appear to extend beyond the women, their children, and their children's children.

Role Failures

At least half of the women have experienced major crises in their lives related to their husbands' behaviors. Of the others, three of the women have never married and six report relatively satisfactory marital relationships, although one of them believes her husband is inadequate as a provider. The ten women who struggled with major marital disturbances are now divorced, separated, or widowed. They report a variety of complaints about their late husbands' behaviors, including alcoholism, infidelity, wife abuse, child abuse, sexual abuse, and criminal activity.

The women report a high incidence of both sexes failing to fulfill the positive family role prescriptions. The litany of family problems the women have endured is staggering. Josie, Judy, Lorraine, and Kitty never knew their fathers; Nancy's father beat her mother and seduced Nancy's sister; Norene's father was in prison, and her step father sexually abused her; Marilyn's step father sexually abused her; Judy's step father tried the same but she left home; Barbara's father was an alcoholic who beat her mother. Marilyn's first husband is serving time for theft; Ida's husband deserted her and their large family of 17 children. Lorraine's husband beat her and finally the children; now an alcoholic drifter, he shows up looking for shelter. Eunice's first husband was an alcoholic; Dorothy's and Reena's husbands drank and then beat them; Cora's husband is blatantly unfaithful.

Kitty's retarded mother gave her to her maternal grandmother to raise; Lorraine's mother had her out of wedlock and gave her to her grandmother as well. Child-like Doris remains dependent on her mother, Eunice, to raise her children; Callie has left her children with Cora and has been charged with prostitution; and Judy's mother has lost custody of her younger children because she did not protect them against their step father's sexual advances.

Yet it is remarkable that all of the women, with the possible exception of Doris, are clear in their minds about how family members should behave and are attempting to live up to their ideals. They are frank about mistakes made by their own mothers and make a conscious effort not to replicate those errors. Grandmothers apparently have provided female role models for some of the women. But the standards for family behavior seem to be so widely accepted in this group that the women understand the rules even in the absence of an immediate positive role model.

Socialization to World Outside of Family

The women have had few opportunities to gain first-hand knowledge of the world outside their immediate family and social circles. Almost all the women stayed with their families until they married or went to live with a man at the median age of 17.5. Their families did not want them to leave home before then, and they believed they should try to please their families. Only two of the women found employment outside the home during the hiatus between school and marriage.

Only one of the women has traveled out of state on her own. Most have never traveled outside Cocke County. Some even feel very anxious if they have to make a trip to Knoxville, a distance of 50 miles. In contrast, local middle-class women say they feel comfortable traveling anywhere within the United States. While the economic circumstances of the lower-status women's lives inhibit much travel away from home, they also are not eager to take advantage of travel opportunities that do become available. When Barbara's husband began to drive her to Nashville to show her where he was working, they got as far as Knoxville when Barbara decided she'd rather return home.

Not only do the low-status women lack worldly experience, this seems to produce a lack of interest in what the world is like outside their own self-imposed boundaries. The researcher sent some of the women postcards from the seashore. When she returned, the women acknowledged her absence but never asked a single question about her experiences. Eunice and Doris, however, are regular viewers of the Phil Donahue show. They quizzed the researcher regarding her opinion on a number of controversial issues such as surrogate mothering and abortion. Their own opinions did not appear to have been affected by the variety of viewpoints presented on the television show and they stayed solidly in the conservative camp. Nancy and Nora put their own interpretation on information from television viewing. They informed the researcher that the hard-to-place and handicapped children up for adoption seen on a weekly news show had "been given up by their mothers just so they could get a man." Their favorite shows were reruns of *Dukes of Hazard* and *Beverly Hillbillies*.

Educational Decisions

The local education system does not appear to have extended the women's general knowledge of or interest in the world outside their families. Only two of the 18 participants completed a high school education. Callie received a GED, and Kitty believes she was only socially promoted and that her education was inadequate. None of the women over 50 had gone further than the eighth grade; they implied that it was far enough to go in their day. This may be representative of their pre-World-War-II cohort. Most of the younger women had quit school in the tenth grade. Ostensible reasons for quitting school included putting family needs before personal ones, wanting to set up housekeeping, marriage or cohabitation, getting pregnant (two pregnancies, both resulting from rape), having a vague but persistent illness, cocky self-assurance that one knows it all, and going to work.

Dropping out of school to help at home may entail providing assistance in caring for a seriously ill relative, caring for younger children, or doing housework or farm work. If a woman in this status group becomes pregnant, marries, or begins to cohabit with a boyfriend, she often quits school. The rural school system does not encourage pregnant women to continue in school, supplying no special programs or counseling. Because most pregnant women do not remain in school, a woman who does will find little peer support. The women believe it is acceptable for a woman to withdraw from activities if she is not physically able to continue. The physical problem need not be clearly defined.

Summary

The most prominent feature in the lives of the women in this study is their bond with their children. The relationship between mothers and adult daughters is particularly strong and includes close physical proximity. Family ties are strong and flexible. Maintaining the intact family unit of parents and children despite all vicissitudes is of high value to most, but not all, of the women. The major alternative family style is a three-generation home, composed of grandmother, mother, and children.

As is typical of rural families in general, the women in this study married relatively early, have more children than the national average, and are likely to live in multi-generational households. Like other rural women they appear to follow traditional sex roles and prefer marriage and motherhood to outside employment. When present, males are expected to provide the economic resources of the family. Although many of the women have experienced family violence, the desertion of a parent, and disappointments in heterosexual relationships, they seem secure in their beliefs about how family roles should be performed and judge themselves accordingly.

CHAPTER FIVE

SOCIAL RELATIONSHIPS

Following is a discussion of how the low-status women in this study perceive their transactions with others in their community. The women have their own sense of social status differentiation and are aware of the differentiations made by higher-status people. Three important social norms emerge from the women's narratives: the norms of reciprocity, equality, and personalized caring.

Awareness of Social Status

The women perceive the local social status hierarchy as a system containing two types of people: those who are in economic positions similar to their own and those who have more money. They believe that having more money does not make a person better. As long as the more economically advantaged person treats the women "just like anyone else," that is, personalizes their interactions and makes no responses that the women deem to be condescending, the low-status women are comfortable with their belief that only an economic difference exists. Higher-status individuals who insist on status privileges are labeled as "snobby people."

In contrast, most middle-status informants, professionals, and clerical workers in the area think there are three social levels: the upper class; the middle class, subdivided into outsiders and locals; and the lower class, subdivided into the diligent and the lazy. (One male interviewee said there were two groups, the "haves" and the "have-nots.") Other studies have varied in such overall class definitions of rural Appalachian groups. Kaplan (1971) identified the "better," "get-by," and "sorry" classes. Stephenson (1968) found four class groups: the top containing full-time employed white collar workers, the middle comprised of full-time employed blue collar workers, the lower-middle of the fairly steadily employed, and the bottom class that is seldom or never employed.

According to the middle-status informants, the upper stratum in Cocke County comprises well-paid professionals (doctors and lawyers) and old families with money and/or land. Most of these people reside in select residential areas in the town of Newport. Membership in this group is not always apparent in appearance and dress. Ostentatious displays of wealth are frowned upon.

The middle stratum is comprised of two groups, the outsiders and the locals. The outsiders are people who have moved into the area either as retirees looking for a pleasant physical environment or as employees of the few national firms that do business in Cocke County. The locals include most of the regularly employed residents. In these families the wife is likely to be employed, and this has enabled the families to weather the recent economic recessions when layoffs have been frequent. Because of the poor employment picture many locals have to "hustle" to bring in needed income. Most hustles are a legal means of using one's skills and abilities in the underground economy, which includes trade and barter as well as money transactions. Some engage in the illegal but profitable business of growing marijuana.

The lower stratum is described by middle-status informants as consisting of two different groups, the diligent and the lazy. The "poor-but-honest" are seen as independent types who have never had much in the way of material goods, are perennially financially strapped but too proud to ask for a handout. The "new" poor are in this category. These are people who have had regular jobs and a taste of the middle-class life style, but have been shut out by the drying up of jobs in the area. They usually have less education and fewer resources than the struggling middle-income worker.

The other group of the poor are "too lazy to work." These are the "dirt poor, on welfare for generations." Some identify the local criminal element as springing from this group. Others remark that this group of people "won't help themselves," or give examples of people on welfare who work for money paid under the table while they draw relief from all available programs (the welfare cheats). The characteristics attributed to this group are congruent with the descriptions of "worthless" folks found in other studies of Appalachia (Beaver, 1976).

Lower-status participants show some awareness of the types of differentiations made by higher-status people. But the lower-status women reject any implication that they, or members of their family, are lazy or not trying hard enough to help themselves. The women usually indicate that they do know "other people" who are not following the behavioral norms of the community, for example, people who cheat, lay out of work, live off someone else, etc., and that they too are indignant about such behavior.

Sensitivity to Status Differences

The women appear to be sensitive to many cues in the context of interactions and become defensive, guarded, angry, hurt, or suspicious when they perceive that their assumptions about the terms of the relationship are violated by the other person. Kitty went to the local church where she has received Christmas baskets in previous years. She said it hurt her feelings the way a woman at the church said there would be no baskets for anyone this year. When questioned further, Kitty added, "She just didn't act like she cared."

The researcher entered the homes of these women as a stranger and an outsider, although she was introduced to most of them by local agency representatives whom they seemed to trust. The researcher was clearly viewed as a person of different status by some of the women who asked her questions about social service resources. Yet many of the women confided sensitive details about their personal lives to her on second and even first visits.

The researcher attempted to observe the etiquette of equality in her dealings with the participants but became aware of how easily persons from outside the area may inadvertently transgress the rules. As she prepared to leave Eunice's home, Eunice said she would cook her a big meal on her next visit. Knowing the limits of Eunice's budget, the researcher demurred, not wanting to take advantage of the participant in any way. Eunice flushed and said heatedly, "Well, my house may not be so clean, but my cooking is good to eat." The researcher realized that when she declined Eunice's offer of hospitality, Eunice assumed she thought she was "too good" to eat with Eunice and had a poor opinion of the cleanliness of the home.

Interactional Expectations

The women in this study have a system of beliefs regarding desirable behaviors in various interpersonal relationships. They judge and measure their own behavior and that of others by these standards. When other people do not fulfill the women's expectations, they experience feelings of injury and/or anger. Such interactions occur in both informal and formal contexts.

In informal interactions with economic and social peers, the women seek emotional and economic reciprocity. Informal interactions take place with family members, extended family and in-laws, peers such as schoolmates, close friends, neighbors, and local tradespeople--people the participants see and interact with on some regular basis.

The women have more ambivalent, quasi-informal interactions with certain higher-status community representatives, such as Child Development workers, who visit in the homes frequently and come to be viewed as friends. Reciprocity is an important factor in all of these relationships.

Formal interactions most often take place with persons of higher social status who are encountered when the women are in the process of obtaining resources and services for their families. This involves interactions with employees of educational, health, welfare, and charitable institutions, as well as with local police, judges, and lawyers. The women occasionally deal with higher-status people from outside the local community, hospitals and doctors in neighboring communities, Social Security agents, and so forth. Most often individuals dealt with in formal interactions occupy a more affluent position in the women's eyes. Not only do these others appear to control access to resources, they appear by their dress, manner, and speech to have more personal resources.

The Importance of Reciprocity

Sociological exchange theorists have pointed to the universal importance of reciprocity in the maintenance of social life (Heath, 1976; Nye, 1982). Heath (1976) differentiates between balanced and generalized reciprocity. Balanced reciprocity contains the expectation that the exchange will be repaid with something of equal value and within a finite time period, with the emphasis on the economic basis of the transaction. In generalized reciprocity the expectation for the return is indefinite and is defined by the social need of the other. Heath (1976) describes generalized reciprocity as "typified by the working-class mother who helps her daughter look after her baby when she is ill and keeps no tally of the debts owed but doubtless expects to be helped herself should she ever need it" (p. 58). Although the giver of a service or favor momentarily assumes a superior status, the relationship is kept in balance by the ability of the other to return the service or favor in kind.

The importance of reciprocity for these women was demonstrated to the researcher during observations of the women in interaction, through stories told by middle-status Child Development workers, and through remarks the women made in a variety of contexts. The women described engaging in both balanced and generalized reciprocity in their informal relationships.

Balanced reciprocity is the process of doing favors for others and returning their favors so that no one appears to have an upper hand in the relationship. The women's economic reciprocity is limited by their lack of money and often takes the form of barter. They share garden produce and home-canned goods with visitors such as Child Development workers. The act of giving an item or extending a service to another may be an advance payment for a favor to be requested. When Norene gave her aunt a beaded necklace, she was wounded when the aunt refused to give her a piece of handwork in return without an exchange of money. Eunice asked if the researcher would help her find employment in Knoxville. Shortly after that request, Eunice offered to fix the researcher a special meal and gave her homemade jelly.

The process of generalized reciprocity appears to be of particular importance to the women's relationships with family members and close friends. When they need help, particularly in caretaking functions such as nursing the sick or raising children, they cannot purchase private services but must count on close associates. Thus they help others as a down payment on future needs. Nancy did heavy yard work for a friend feeling she was repaying her for her willingness to provide transportation for Nancy and her children both in the past and the future. Mothers who periodically provide a home for their adult children and their families expect to find a home eventually with these children when they no longer can live independently.

Another form of reciprocity occurs in informal interactions when the women feel the other has given them a negative interchange. In these cases, the women actively plan how they will pay the other back in kind. How many of these planned revenges take place is unknown, but the women are convinced they will find an opportunity to get even. One of Norene's church friends commented that Norene "did not have the good sense of a two-year-old." Norene is still rehearsing her retort.

The Etiquette of Equality

A reliance on an ethic of egalitarianism and expectations of personalized treatment have been described as characteristic of Appalachians. Beaver (1986) suggests that the necessity for maintaining cooperative behaviors in small rural communities has engendered the belief that all people are accepted and equal. Despite the fact that social distinctions have been present in Appalachian rural communities for generations, the observance of the egalitarian ethic persists in local social customs.

The women in this study possess a well-developed sense of etiquette for this type of interaction, an etiquette of equality. Their sense of fairness demands that they be accorded the same services available to others regardless of economic or social status and that they be treated as equals. The other person's behaviors and/or their non-verbal communication may imply to the women that they are in some sense being rejected, criticized, or scorned. If it seems to them that someone believes them to be inferior, the women feel put down. But at the same time, they believe the other has a problem and should change their behavior. Eunice was angry when she thought that nurses in the emergency room were usurping the doctor's role and "asking me questions like the doctor should ask. I let them know right then that I intended to see the doctor." She attributes this behavior to the fact that she has a Medicaid card and thus is a charity case. "You better believe the nurses and doctors would act different if I came in with a $50 bill."

When others put on airs, or act as if they are better than the women, they transgress the rules of egalitarian relationships. Those who are members of higher status groups, such as the middle-class Child Development workers, are expected to minimize the differences between themselves and the low-status women. Cora's town friend, who has plenty of money and a nice house, broke this rule when she said she "had better things to do with her time than visit (Cora) way out in the country," thus emphasizing the social distance between them.

The women are sensitive to criticism that implies they (or a family member) are not performing appropriately or adequately and thus may be held in low esteem. The women believe that they have been behaving correctly and doing their best and are indignant when others imply differently. Often the women are in the process of fulfilling one of their major self-expectations, that of providing for the needs of their children and other family members, when they encounter such criticism. Cora believes she manages her large family well and became indignant when she thought her food-stamp worker was implying that "she (the worker) would not have any trouble feeding a family on *that* amount of stamps without running out of food" as Cora sometimes does. Implied criticism of family members is also taken as an insult. Mary was furious that the surplus food worker implied her husband was lazy and had not really looked for work.

This feeling is particularly keen when the women believe their peers are putting them down for reasons over which they have no control. The women do not deny that they possess the attribute germane to the put-down, but feel rejected because some attribute integral to their self has been deemed inferior. Caren felt so put down by the other girls at school who teased her about her placement in special education resource classes that she dropped out of school. Josie was not comfortable or happy after she began to attend the large county high school. She thought schoolmates who had more economic resources made too much of their differences from the poorer youngsters. This was one of the reasons she gave for dropping out of school. Josie's mother had not been married and her children were raised on welfare.

Personalization and Caring

The personalizing of relationships among Appalachians, particularly low-status people, has often been viewed in negative terms. Weller (1965) states, "Because the mountain man finds his self-identification mainly in his relationship with others, he has never developed a satisfactory self-image as a single individual" (p. 83-84). Weller refers to the man's ". . . inability to relate to persons on other than a personal basis" (p. 84). From his perspective, Appalachians cannot deal with the impersonal or hostile behaviors of others because the mere hint of criticism threatens basic feelings about self.

A more benign view is held by Brown and Schwarzweller (1974) who theorize that personalism and belief in equality have a similar source in Appalachian history as accommodations to pressure created to maintain kin networks. Pearsall (1974) notes the prevalence of personalism in other rural or isolated societies. She finds that rural people are more likely to base their reactions and behaviors on how they are treated in a situation than on an overall appraisal of situational factors.

> Whether a patient stays in a hospital or leaves against medical advice depends more on his personal relations with hospital personnel than on any understanding he may have of his medical condition and the hospital's technical competence in treating him. (p. 61)

The women in this study expect that others with whom they interact will take a personal interest in them and their family members. They feel put down when they believe they are being dealt with in an impersonal or stereotyped fashion. When others do not seem to take notice of the women's particular needs they may feel scorned or rejected. Because they feel they would be sensitive to the needs of others if the roles were reversed, they think their needs are apparent and do not need to be defined. When Cora stayed in a Knoxville hospital with her grandson, she had no money for food nor a place to sleep. She was incredulous that the nurses, a generic term for women in white, had not shown any interest in her situation as she remained at the bedside day after day. In these contexts the women are sensitive to the manner of other's communications. Cora thought the nurses stereotyped her when they did communicate with her. She notes that the women kept repeating the home care instructions to her as if she was some type of "dumb country woman," but she did not see them acting that way with city women.

Because the women see their interactions as personal in nature they expect their honesty to be accepted on principle. Marilyn became distraught and angry when her HUD worker would not believe that Marilyn's ex-husband was not living with her, which would be a breach of her rental contract.

In their own eyes, these women attempt to honor the etiquette of equality and personal caring in their interactions with others. They believe they are sympathetic to other people and do not "put on airs," or "act like they are better than others." They accept other people as they present themselves and are only critical of others who they feel have put them down.

Dealing With Feeling Put Down

The women's belief in the community norm of equality and their commitment to their social roles in their families appears to aid them when faced with what they perceive as unfair criticism. They are confident they are right. Whether they take an active or passive stance toward the critic depends on their personality style. Some women defend themselves against criticism by letting others know they disagree with their assessment of them. Eunice describes her feelings when she believes others are putting her down. She says her feelings just "well up" and she can feel the pressure of them in her chest. When that happens she just has to say something to the other person and apparently she will "give them an earful." But Eunice adds that she only does this "up to a point." She seems to have a sense of how much of a hostile retort another person will take before retaliating. And because these others may play a role in providing access to resources or services for the women, retaliation is to be avoided.

Some women keep silent in the face of perceived unjust criticism, but they fashion a justification for their own perception of the situation and append this to the telling of the incident to sympathetic listeners. Cora decided the food-stamp worker did not know about living in poverty and feeding a large family. "You have to have lived it to understand it," Cora justifies herself.

The most common response to situations in which the women do not believe they can do anything to affect the negatively perceived behaviors or attitudes of others is silence and withdrawal from the situation as soon as possible. Keeping their feelings of unfair treatment to themselves, the women retreat to the safety of their families. But they retell the story of the unhappy interaction to family members, neighbors, and sympathetic others, seeking justification and support for their own behavior.

In some instances, the women seek out someone who might have sufficient power to defend them or to right the wrong they feel. Marilyn decided to go to Legal Aid when she was unable to convince her HUD worker that her ex-husband was not spending the night with her, which was grounds for eviction. Marilyn believed the HUD worker was retaliating against her for going over her head to get the present trailer she rents--perhaps a type of negative reciprocity. When the Department of Human Services refused to return custody of Shirley's children because they suspected abuse was occurring during home visits, she filed a petition in court, hoping the local judge would see her side of the story. He did not.

Some of the women in this study defend themselves by attaching a negative label to the others' behaviors. Thus when others break the women's social rule regarding equality in interactions, they may be labeled "snobby people" or "people who put on airs." In the women's opinion, even individuals who do have higher social standing and more economic resources should know that they are not supposed to call attention to their status and certainly not at the expense of those who have less. Some women feel this so keenly that they will give up advantages for themselves rather than be associated with snobby people. When Barbara was promoted to the fast-learning group in middle school she left most of her status peers behind. When she heard how the higher-status students teased and talked about the slower learners, mostly her old friends, Barbara decided she did not want to remain in the group. Her personalized view of how people should treat others was her guide, and she did not believe that the advantages of remaining in the fast group should outweigh her loyalty to her friends.

Discussion

The women in the study seem to use interactional modes that are common in their Appalachian setting. But an important dynamic in their lives, from their perspective, is the frequency with which these interactional norms seem to be broken by others with higher social standing. Two questions come to the mind of the observer. Do the women really sustain more put-downs than women in other social strata, or are the women more sensitive or suspicious in their dealings with others? This study cannot answer these questions in a definitive fashion, but it does supply some information germane to their consideration.

The opportunities for perceiving social put downs should increase with the number of interactions a low-status person has with higher-status individuals. Certainly the daily lives of these women are rife with opportunities of this sort. The search for services and resources for their families brings them into contact with employees of social agencies, most of whom would define themselves as having a higher social standing than the applicants for their agency services. During the five months of this study, the participants were involved in obtaining services or resources from nineteen different local or regional community agencies. These usually involved trips to offices, time spent in waiting rooms, or waiting lines. (See Appendix for summary of agencies contacted) The women did not encounter criticism, rejection, or scorn in their contacts with individuals in all the service sectors enumerated. But given the numbers of people they interact with every month, including receptionists, clerks, and professionals in each setting, the risk of feeling slighted in the exchanges is considerable.

As a participant observer in some of the community agencies serving low-status women, the researcher overheard random negative comments about specific low-status people and the poor in general. One agency person told the researcher that they did not like a male recipient of their services because he let his wife do all the work, but he kept on siring her children. The worker said they had taken the husband to task, claiming he had misused a service and implying he would not receive help again although he was eligible for further service.

It is not feasible from the women's accounts of the put-down incidents to determine the intent of the others in the interactions, nor to ascertain whether the women are hypersensitive to slights. The expectation that relationships will be personalized is, however, a prescription for disappointment and hurt feelings for people entering large and impersonal social systems. Therefore, low-status Appalachian women may be more sensitive to put-downs in places like big city hospitals and clinics. The anxiety that many of the women associate with being so far from home may also play a role in their sensitivity to the behaviors of others.

Attitudes about the deserving versus the undeserving poor appear to override the traditional egalitarianism of the region for some middle-status locals. The mixture of attitudes in the local community, about why people are poor and why they remain so, does set the stage for what the women perceive as snobby behavior. How the women deal with social put downs and maintain a positive sense of self will be discussed in the next chapter.

CHAPTER SIX

FEELINGS ABOUT SELF

The previous chapter discussed the interactions between the women of this study and others in their social environment, as perceived by the participants. When the women believe they have been treated unfairly or as inferiors by others, they describe feelings of injury and anger. Interactions that produce such negative feelings seem to occur regularly in the women's lives. An analysis of the women's self-perceptions reveals that while negative interchanges with close family members may lead to bad feelings about self, the women are able to maintain positive self-appraisals in the face of perceived put downs from higher-status people.

The very mores that render the women vulnerable to feelings of being put down, a belief in egalitarianism and the personalization of all relationships, also serve to protect their self-evaluations. For as long as they believe that they live up to these standards of behavior, the women can feel good about their own performances. Their adherence to their family and gender role as mothers is the other essential part of their self-appraisal. By remaining within the boundaries of their role prescriptions the women receive both internal and external reinforcement for their activities.

The most serious threat to the development of positive feelings about self among these women was a history of childhood sexual abuse, specifically incestuous behavior. Feelings of self-esteem may be damaged in abusive intimate relationships, but positive feelings are regained when such relationships are terminated.

Although the scope of the women's lives is a narrow one, largely limited to their families, particularly their children, they are generally able to maintain positive self-images as they fulfill their expectations as mothers and find small ways to express their individuality. This chapter will first examine how the women use their view of their family role performance to express positive feelings about themselves. Next the negative self-images projected by a few of the women will be discussed. And, finally, the personal characteristics and accomplishments the women value in themselves will be detailed.

Self-Esteem and Family Role Performance

The women are completely absorbed by the details of their daily lives in which their children are the central part. Almost all of their energies are directed toward obtaining the basic necessities for their families. Few have any prospects of this changing either because they are supported by welfare or have other limited sources of income. The exceptions are male-headed households where the potential for employment is higher.

Doing Right

The women use their belief that they are "doing right" by their children to sustain positive self-feelings. When women meet their standards for being a good mother (accepting all pregnancies, ensuring the children's basic needs are met, putting the children's needs first, protecting the children from harm, accepting the children unconditionally, and providing a proper model for their children) they consider themselves successes. These mothers do not feel responsible for molding their children's intellectual development, nor do they judge their own performance by their children's achievements. Rather they conceptualize their role as a succession of caretaking tasks related to the physical well-being of the children and as a life long responsibility.

The women have definite opinions about the process of raising children and take pride in sharing their child-rearing wisdom. The general pattern for raising children centers on providing them care and protection. Infants are indulged, remaining on the bottle well into their second year. Once beyond the toddler stage, children are expected to become more independent and the most common form of punishment, following lengthy verbal threats, is the application of small switches or soft belts to whatever part of the child's anatomy is handy.

Feelings About Self

When faced with people from a higher social stratum the women may become defensive about late weaning and physical punishment or recite middle-status toilet training procedures in response to their perception of the other's expectations. But the women know how they want their children to behave and what is important to them. It is important to Barbara that her children be able to stand up for themselves, and she does not interfere when her oldest daughter picks on the little ones, for she wants them to learn to defend themselves. She is firm in her adherence to this policy and defies the opinions of both her husband and father-in-law, who live in the home. Nora is proud of her grandchildren's quiet behavior in autos. She has trained them not disturb the driver.

The women express pride in their own performance when they believe they have surmounted uncommon obstacles in order to care properly for their children. Ida knew she was in for hard times when her husband deserted her for another woman and left Ida to raise their seventeen children on a poor rural farm. She had no medical insurance when five of the children "came down with the pneumonia fever." (This was prior to the enactment of Medicaid benefits.) She nursed them all at home, using some herbal remedies and the help of the country doctor whom she paid with her cherry crop. Nearing 70 Ida is the respected matriarch of her family and is raising her great grand-daughter. Her whole life is centered in her family.

Reena's statement, "My children mean everything to me," expresses the value which ultimately guided her through years of sorrow. Reena had wanted nothing more than to be a good wife and mother when she married at 17. By the time she had six children she was living in a small, isolated trailer with an alcoholic husband who beat her and stole all the family's resources to buy liquor. She tried to protect her children from the physical abuse and to find enough food for them even if it meant begging when she could get to town. But she knew that this way of living was not right and that her younger children had become terrified of their father. Still she felt powerless to do anything until the Department of Human Services took her oldest daughter into custody, claiming incest, and threatened to place the other children as well.

Reena had nowhere to go, but she was determined to keep her children. She left that day with little except the children and with the help of the Department of Human Services' Homemaker, Reena found a small house to rent and began to receive Aid to Families with

Dependent Children. She still lived in fear of her husband, but slowly she learned to do for herself and the children all the tasks she had once expected her husband to perform. Reena has recently married a second time. She has also gained the mature confidence that she can make it on her own again if need be.

The importance of feeling that one is a good mother was demonstrated by Callie, a women who, to all appearances, seems to have failed as a mother up to this point. Callie was raped and then married before she was 16 years old. She is now divorced, and her children have been in her mother's custody while Callie lived in another state. Her mother, Cora, speaks disapprovingly of Callie's drinking and promiscuous behavior since her divorce. During the course of this study, Callie returned to her mother's home, immediately resumed physical responsibility for her children, got a part-time job, and began to talk of saving money for her own trailer and a water hookup so she could regain custody of her children. No one in her family appears to have insisted that Callie attempt to resume her role as mother to her children. It seemed to be important to her sense of self. But Callie was unable to live up to the standards she knew must be met, and she drifted back to bars in town.

Negative Feelings About Self

Sexual Abuse

Norene and Marilyn reflect predominantly negative feelings about themselves, and both women feel their lives have been in constant turmoil. The women attribute their present unhappiness to their feelings about being sexually abused by their stepfathers. Callie, whose promiscuous behavior cost her the custody of her children, has also been abused by a male family member.

These adult women are filled with anger toward the step fathers who raped and had continuing sexual relations with them. Marilyn feels she did not really have a father. She never knew her natural father and of her step father she says, "I don't count him as a real father because of what he did to me." Allied with this feeling are the women's perceptions that their mothers failed when they were either unwilling or unable to prevent the abuse. Thus the bad father's behavior produced an estrangement between mother and daughter as well, disrupting the closest emotional tie that most low-status women develop.

This type of injury seems to be permanent and to have a negative and pervasive effect on the women's lives. The men's mistreatment of them is held responsible for problems the women have in fulfilling their self-expectations in the present. Norene believes that her step father's abuse and her continuing anger toward her non-protecting mother is the cause of the recurring depressions that require hospitalization and interfere with her desire to be a good wife and mother. After multiple marriages, Marilyn despairs of finding a "good man" and blames this on her abusive step father who, she believes, is still "pulling the strings" in her life.

Abused Wives

Women who have been abused by their husbands also report experiencing negative feelings about their self-worth during the marriage. But once removed from the violent relationship, they speak of regaining their self-respect.

Eight of the women report they have been physically abused by a husband at some point in their lives. Most of them look back on that period of their life as a nightmare. They believe they stayed so long (almost always years) because they thought that was what they were supposed to do. They were trying to fulfill their family roles, be good wives, keep the family together, please their men, protect their children, and they were always hopeful the men would provide the economic base for their survival. Some were puzzled when their efforts to be good wives were not rewarded, so they tried harder. Some speak of having feelings of failure after they left that persisted for some time.

These women also believe they were demeaned and psychologically abused when their men disparaged their skills and abilities. The women say they accepted their mates' evaluations of them until they came to reject their mates for other reasons. Lorraine's husband had told her, "Nobody would want you," when she talked about going to work. She said that she accepted that dim view of herself until she realized her husband was unfaithful, and she began her attempts to make him move out of their house.

The women who disentangle themselves from dependent and abusive relationships see that they have changed their life course.

Lorraine calls this process "getting backbone." She says that when she was married to her unfaithful and abusive husband who told her no one else would have her, she used to just "hump up to life," taking life's blows. When asked how she got backbone, Lorraine said it was through the hatred she developed for her husband. First, she refused to have further sexual relations with him. Then she demanded that he move out of the home. He has accused her of alienating their children from him, but she replied that he had condemned himself through his own actions. She has never had the money for a divorce, but what is important to her is that she knows she is free.

The women in this study do not think that they deserve to be abused physically or psychologically. They do imply that at the time, they felt they must not be living up to their men's expectations for a wife, and thus they tried harder while tolerating the male behavior.

Allied to their desire to live up to their expectations was their perception that there were few alternatives. They were raised to depend on their mates for economic survival, had no marketable skills, little experience of the outside world, and no place else to go. Returning to their parental home was usually not a viable alternative because it also had sparse resources. As Reena said, "My mom still had the other young ones to raise." Families are also reluctant to become involved in disputes between spouses because such interference could backfire if the partners reconciled.

The injuries to feelings about self emphasized by these women, which occur in the course of their primary relationships with family members, are the result of behaviors that are not uncommon in families in other social strata. And despite the painfulness of such experiences, all of the women, except those who were sexually abused, were able to recount how they regained their self-esteem once they removed themselves from the abusive situation.

Endurance and the Little Things in Life

The women reveal positive feelings about themselves related both to personal characteristics and to their view of their accomplishments. They are proud when they believe they have persevered in hard times and exercised some control over some aspects of their life. Although this is not a cultural group in which people "toot their own horns," the women do like to demonstrate their skills and accomplishments, albeit often indirectly.

Independence of Mind

The women are pleased with themselves when they believe they are the kind of person who does not give up. They speak of efforts to tackle tasks in the face of failure or of doing what is needed despite obstacles. Types of perseverance and the credit women take for their efforts depend on where they are in their struggles.

Some women can reflect on how difficult it was to keep trying when so much seemed to be against them. Ida's stories of raising her seventeen children after her husband's desertion are of this type. Other women are in the midst of trying to do something where they have no assurance they can succeed, but they keep trying. Lorraine is in her mid-fifties and afraid of water, but she goes back each summer to take swimming lessons with her grandchildren, determined to learn the skill. Some women keep trying although they almost lose heart. Kitty has been trying for over a year through a variety of appeals to establish her youngest child's eligibility for SSI payments. That additional income will mean the difference between having a trailer of their own or continuing to live with relatives. She calls Social Security weekly and watches the mail anxiously. She has not given up, but some days she feels discouraged.

The women feel good about themselves when they believe they are responsible and in charge of at least some of the important aspects of their lives. In their perception they are instrumental in shaping at least a part of their destiny. This sense of agency takes various forms.

Some of the younger women are proud that they have not allowed men to abuse them as their mothers have been abused. These women are confident that, unlike their mothers, they will leave a relationship if the male becomes abusive. Nancy is not even sure she ever wants to marry and take the risk of mistreatment.

Some women believe they have an independence of mind that establishes their sense of agency in life. Independent-mindedness was defined by one woman as not taking orders from others. This does not necessarily mean the women directly confront others. Rather an independent-minded woman knows how to bargain to gain her point. When Barbara was first married, her husband was against her reading so many books and wanted her to stop. She said she'd stop if he'd give up something of comparable value. They could not decide on what that something would be. Finally, her husband gave up his demand and bought her a box of books at the flea market.

A few of the women have found that their ability to competently fill an occupational role as well as a maternal/conjugal role makes them feel empowered. These women say they feel best when they are working outside the home. They are invigorated by their interactions in the larger world and find that they have more energy to complete their usual tasks at home. Although these women will usually terminate their employment at their husband's request, they do not forget the positive image employment provided them and have plans to return to work later.

Recognizing Accomplishments

The women take pride in their accomplishments and readily demonstrate or talk about these to available audiences. Most of their accomplishments are achieved in the context of their home environment. The home is the only sphere where many of these women have any opportunity to exercise their skills. Rural isolation, inability to drive a vehicle, or lack of reliable transportation limit the women's environment. Some women report that their husbands or boyfriends would not teach them how to drive. This acts as a cultural restraint imposed by some men which supports the continued patriarchal control of these women's lives. Thus, learning to drive a car is an accomplishment to crow about. Ida's husband "never let her around his cars," but after her divorce, Ida, then in her fifties, learned how to drive and "got my license on the first try while my friend had to go there four times."

Some women proudly point out their home activities while others bring these to a visitor's attention indirectly. When Edna and Dorothy moved to a new rental home, Edna (the grandmother) cleared the backyard of brush and began to adapt an old shed for her chicken coop. The researcher was taken on a tour of her accomplishments. In contrast, Nancy spoke through her two-year-old who was pointing to the many pictures and illustrations tacked to their wooden walls. "Tell the lady who painted those (paint-by-the-numbers) pictures," she said. "Mamma," came the reply. Other women show visitors shelves of newly canned

Feelings About Self

foods or talk about their gardens past and present. Other skills the women claim include house repairs, helping a mate build their home, growing tobacco, raising animals, and generally managing to make ends meet on limited resources.

A few women count as an accomplishment the ability to transcend their limited physical environments. They believe they are more knowledgeable about the world in general because they have "been other places." Ida attributes her superior knowledge of the world to living in a mill town in North Carolina in her childhood. Her relatives and neighbors come to her for advice on many matters. After her divorce, Lorraine got up the courage to go all by herself to visit relatives in a distant state.

Summary

Positive feelings about self were expressed by most of the women in this study. They felt good about "doing the right thing." This involves meeting their commitments to their children and never acting like they are better than the next person. Although these positive feelings about themselves may be lost in the course of an abusive relationship, the women demonstrate resilience once they terminate such relationships. Only the women who were abused as children appear to have permanent damage to their self feelings. Within the boundaries of their family-centered lives, the women take pride in their achievements and accomplishments.

The women's ability to maintain positive feelings about themselves does need to be viewed within their larger social context, for they maintain this vital coping capacity in the face of many negative situational factors. As detailed in Chapter Three, all of these women live in poverty. They never cease struggling to make ends meet. Many live in inadequate housing. They must constantly interact with impersonal social institutions in which some personnel offend the women's sense of equity. And the women's hope for family stability is dependent on the ability of the men in their status group to find employment and make family commitments.

CHAPTER SEVEN

SUMMARY AND IMPLICATIONS

Summary of Findings

This research was developed to gain knowledge regarding the social reality of low-status Appalachian women. Specifically, how does a group of these women perceive themselves and their social world? What are the values and beliefs that direct their behavior? Existing studies of low-status women present conflicting pictures of such women and contain little information regarding the women's point of view. As a means of gaining access to such information, this study was conducted using qualitative methods, participant observation, and unstructured interviews and was centered on visits with 18 rural women in 14 households. The resulting data were analyzed using grounded theory method, coding the data for categories of meaning, and developing the linkages among categories.

Three primary areas of social process emerged that aided in defining the women's construction of their world: the belief system that directs the women's family role behavior, the morality that directs the conduct of their interpersonal interactions, and the construction of their self-appraisals. The dynamics of this social process are as follows: the women take for granted their participation in traditional female family roles and the egalitarian nature and personalization of all social interactions. This perspective leaves the women situationally vulnerable due to two factors: first, economic conditions that threaten family formation and stability and, second, the necessity of engaging in multiple impersonal and unequal interactions in the search for economic resources for their families. Most of the women maintain positive feelings about themselves by confining their self-evaluations to their family role performance, their ability to persevere, and their equitable treatment of others.

The life style of these low-status women is not unique nor does it appear to be a specific adaptation to the conditions of poverty that are an ever-present part of their lives. They are in tune with the values and beliefs of their rural community. In their adherence to traditional female family roles, the women are similar to rural women everywhere who have less access to new role options. The dominance of the mother-daughter bond and the women's emphasis on the centrality of child care to their lives are characteristic of low-status women elsewhere in American culture. The women's morality of equality has roots in past Appalachian culture.

The Nuclear Family Ideal

This study highlights, however, some aspects of the women's view of their world that are either absent from or contradictory to earlier descriptions. The primacy of the nuclear family in middle-status society versus the importance of the extended family in lower-status social groups is a recurring theme in social science literature (Schneider & Smith, 1973). Although it is true that the majority of the women in this study were not living in nuclear family units, it is important to understand that the nuclear family unit is their ideal and the fantasy they carry into adulthood. They attribute their inability to achieve this ideal to the failure of the men in their lives either to find the means to economically support a family or to avoid antisocial behaviors, specifically alcoholism and violent behavior. Involvement with their extended family is not central in their lives, and multiple living arrangements seldom extend beyond mothers and their adult children's families.

The Egalitarian Ideal

The women do demonstrate what has been called traditional mountain women values: cooperativeness and egalitarianism (Lewis, Kobak, & Johnson, 1978). They also personalize all of their interactions. The researcher did not find that these values differed, however, from those held by many middle-status individuals in the community. Interactions between individuals in this rural community, regardless of status group, follow an etiquette that requires recognition of each person's identity through acknowledgement of either their social role or family connections and calls for egalitarian conduct.

The women feel injured when they think they have been put down in an interaction, and may withdraw. This study found that, contrary to descriptions of this as passive or fatalistic behavior, there is considerable anger and self-righteousness in the women's reactions. They are indignant or incredulous when others break social contracts. They seek comfort in the assurance that they are behaving correctly and the other is at fault. This may be the reason behind the women's frequent telling of stories about social insults, for in the retelling they are free to present the righteousness of their own behavior and the undesirable snobbishness of the other.

Self-Appraisals

The women in this study have positive self-appraisals based on their performance as mothers, which supports Fitchen's (1981) conclusion that low-status women are able to attain their role ideals as wives and mothers particularly when compared to men in their social group who become frustrated in their roles as providers. But the more subtle means by which these women add to their self-esteem have seldom been noted. They value their competencies and small achievements even while recognizing that others may not.

When low-status women are viewed both within their environmental context and on the basis of their perception of reality, the psychological characteristics attributed to them in earlier studies, overconformity, inexpressiveness, and fatalism, seem too limited (Polansky et al., 1972; Looff, 1971). Conformity takes on new meaning when it is seen that adherence to the traditional mothering role is a source of positive self-feelings for these women. Inexpressiveness may be a characteristic of some families in this region but could not be applied to the majority of the women in this study. In reviewing the course of their lives, the women do report feeling fatalistic about some events and life situations, accepting these as God's will or as unchangeable. But the same women grasp opportunities to change these very situations and value highly their ability to exert some independence or control. An awareness of the women's perspective can enrich our present understanding and provide the knowledge essential for the destruction of stereotypical images and class-biased views of the world of low-status women.

Implications

Developing an understanding of how women in a specific social stratum and a particular environment conceive the reality of their lives has implications on two levels for social work practitioners and program planners. First, it presents a model for increasing the practitioners' knowledge of the world of their clients and how this world differs substantially from the practitioners' reality. Such knowledge is essential to the process of aiding individuals and groups in solving life problems. Second, such an understanding provides the basis for tailoring general social programs to meet the perceived needs of specific population groups.

Knowledge for Practice

One of the basic directives to social work practitioners is to "start where the client is." While such an approach refers to clients' views of the problem, their particular strengths and weaknesses, and what they desire from the practitioner, it also implies understanding the clients in their social context. This requires the practitioner to make a series of assumptions about the client's beliefs and values and customary ways of interacting, often with only minimal evidence. The practitioner is often reduced to using social categories based on demographic norms. Age, sex, race, occupation, and income are frequently the only data available for developing such an understanding.

The method used in this study, however, offers an alternative route for securing a deeper understanding of the client's world. This consists of analyzing the clients' stories about their lives, analyzing them for the underlying themes and the meanings clients attribute to events. It can provide a means of examining the cultural prescriptions that direct clients' behaviors. Tentative conclusions regarding clients' constructions of their social worlds can be verified and modified or discarded as needed. The ability of the practitioner to reflect back to clients such an enhanced understanding of their world should have a positive effect on the helping relationship. It may also assist clients in developing a more holistic way of seeing their life space.

An understanding of the rules that govern social interactions for given clients may assist a practitioner in avoiding interventions that are incongruous within the client's reality. Certainly it should guide the practitioner's relational style. For example, the women discussed in this study would be uncomfortable with a practitioner who stood on formalities and insisted on calling them by a formal title after their initial meeting.

Program Planning and Service Delivery

Social workers employed in administrative and planning roles can also benefit from knowledge gained from grounded theory studies of specific social group values and interactional expectations. Studies of this type point to areas where situational stress and institutional practices impede client functioning. They also alert the planner to the fact that programs must be flexible enough to adapt to pertinent local situations.

The current call for welfare reform at the national level includes provision of some type of "workfare" for welfare recipients. What would be the impact of such program requirements on the women in this study who are dependent on public monies? It is likely that without an appreciation of both the women's guiding beliefs and the salient factors in their environment, such a program could do harm and accomplish little more than the creation of more middle-class, bureaucratic jobs.

At the individual level, employment would be feasible and positive if it does not jeopardize the women's belief in their ability to do right by their children. This will require the provision of low-cost day care and after-school programs staffed by personnel prepared to personalize their interactions with the parents. It will require employers who accept the fact that no self-respecting mother in this group will leave a very ill child with other caretakers even if a job depends on it.

The women will require job training programs that are close to home and include the provision for additional economic support. If the women's days are to be spent in training or employment, they will no longer be able to make the regular rounds in search of the community resources on which they depend to augment their small welfare allowances. If this resource gap cannot be closed, the women will undoubtedly begin to drop out of the program. Driving lessons and low-interest loans for the purchase of cars will be needed by a sizeable number of women in order to make employment feasible.

An alternative approach might be an extensive development of handcraft cooperatives, a model for which currently exists in a few Appalachian counties. Training interested women to produce craft items in their own homes for the tourist market could obviate some of the women's concerns regarding leaving their young children to go away to work. These are just some of the more community-specific concerns that would enhance the probability of success in introducing new jobs programs aimed at this population group.

Findings of studies of this type can be useful in community and regional planning done on a more systemic level. The needs of specific population groups are important when dealing with comprehensive economic planning. For example, the economic well-being of most women in this study has been tied directly to the ability of the men in their status group to find and hold employment that pays wages above the poverty level. A jobs program that addressed this issue might have a longer-range effect on the stability of family life for these women than any change in welfare benefits.

Mental health planners can use data of this type in ascertaining the type of clinical services that would be utilized by this population group such as early intervention for victims of child abuse and alternative resources for victims of family violence. They can also explore the kind of family-life educational programs that could enhance their clients' coping skills.

Further Research

Grounded theory research is just beginning to emerge in the social work profession, and the breadth of its applicability is still to be tested. This study took a holistic approach by studying the general construction of social reality in a specific status group. But the method should be equally applicable to looking at the interactional context of individuals, families, and small groups within clinical settings and the interactional rules of organizational structures of concern to social work.

APPENDIX

Programs and Services Used by Participants During the Study

A. Economic Resource Services

1. Aid to Families with Dependent Children, Department of Human Services, eligibility determination may include a journey to Knoxville for blood tests as part of a requirement to force absent fathers to provide child support
2. Food stamps, Department of Human Services
3. Community Action Office, food commodities and utility and emergency food vouchers as needed
4. Social Security office
5. Housing and Urban Development office, rental assistance, includes home visits by agency worker
6. Housing projects

B. Services for Children
1. Women, Infants, and Children, Public Health Department or Child Health and Development Program, a nutrition program for pregnant women and children under 5 years of age, provides vouchers for specific food stuffs
2. Pediatric care, doctor's offices, local hospital emergency room, Public Health office
3. Hospital care, local and in Knoxville
4. Head Start, transportation provided in some parts of the county

B. Services for Children

　　5. TOPS, a special day program for developmentally delayed preschoolers, provides transportation
　　6. Child Health and Development, largely a home-based program but includes an office appointment every 3 months
　　7. Specialty clinics in Knoxville, including Crippled Children's Services, UT Speech and Hearing Center, UT Birth Defects Center

C. Health Services

　　1. Prenatal care, local hospital clinic or Public Health Department, home visits and transportation sometimes provided by Department of Human Services
　　2. Family planning clinic, Public Health Department
　　3. Mental Health Clinic
　　4. Local doctors

D. Involuntary Services

　　1. Protective services, Department of Human Services, home investigation of complaints of abuse or neglect
　　2. Homemaker, home based service to increase compliance with protective service goals

REFERENCES

Abramovitz, M. (1986). Social policy and the female pauper: The family ethic in the U.S. Welfare State. In N.V.D. Bergh & L.B. Cooper (Eds.), *Feminist visions for social work* (pp. 211-228). Silver Springs, MD: National Association of Social Workers.

Agar, M.H. (1980). *The professional stranger: An informal introduction to ethnography.* New York: Academic Press.

Agar, M.H. (1986). *Speaking of ethnography.* Beverly Hills: Sage.

Allen, V.L. (1970). Personality correlates of poverty. In V.L. Allen (Ed.), *Psychological factors in poverty* (pp. 242-266). Chicago: Markham.

Anson, R.S. (1981). Some of the finest Christian people you'll ever want to meet. *Esquire, 95*(6), 44-51.

Ball, R.A. (1968). A poverty case: The analgesic subculture of the southern Appalachians. *American Sociological Review, 33,* 885-895.

Bealer, R.C., Willits, F.W., & Kuvlesky, W.P. (1965). The meaning of "rurality" in American society: Some implications of alternative definitions. *Rural Sociology, 30*(3), 255-266.

Beaver, P.D. (1976). *Symbols and social organization in an Appalachian community.* Unpublished doctoral dissertation, Duke University, Durham, NC.

Beaver, P.D. (1986). *Rural community in the Appalachian south.* Lexington: University Press of Kentucky.

Berger, P.L., & Luckmann, T. (1967). *The social construction of reality: A treatise in the sociology of knowledge.* Garden City, NY: Anchor Books.

Bernard, J. (1981). *The female world.* New York: Free Press.

Bernstein, B., & Henderson, D. (1973). Social class differences in the relevance of language to socialization. In B. Bernstein (Ed.), *Class, codes, and control: Vol. 2, Applied studies toward a sociology of language* (pp. 24-47). London: Routledge & Kegan Paul.

Bescher-Donnelly, L., & Smith, L.W. (1981). The changing roles and status of rural women. In R.T. Coward & W.M. Smith Jr. (Eds.), *The family in rural society* (pp. 167-185). Boulder, CO: Westview.

Billings, D. (1974). Culture and poverty in Appalachia: A theoretical discussion and empirical analysis. *Social Forces, 53*, 315-323.

Bronfenbrenner, U. (1958). Socialization and social class through time and space. In E.E. Maccoby, T.M. Newcomb, & E.L. Hartley (Eds.), *Readings in social psychology* (3rd ed., pp. 400-425). New York: Henry Holt.

Brown. D.L. (1981). A quarter century of trends and changes in the demographic structure of American families. In R.T. Coward & W.M. Smith Jr. (Eds.), *The family in rural society* (pp. 9-25). Boulder, CO: Westview.

Brown, J.S., & Schwarzweller, H.K. (1974). The Appalachian family. In F.S. Riddel (Ed.), *Appalachia: Its people, heritage, and problems* (pp. 63-75). Dubuque: Kendall/Hunt.

Buss, F.L. (1985). *Lower income women tell of their lives and struggles*. Ann Arbor, MI: University of Michigan Press.

Cavender, A. (1981). *An ethnographic inquiry into social identity, social stratification, and premature school withdrawal in a rural Appalachian school*. Unpublished doctoral dissertation, University of Tennessee, Knoxville, TN.

Chenitz, W.C., & Swanson, J.M. (1986). Qualitative research using grounded theory. In W.C. Chenitz & J.M. Swanson (Eds.), *From practice to grounded theory: Qualitative research in nursing* (pp. 3-15). Menlo Park, CA: Addison Wesley.

Chilman, C.S.(1968). Poor families and their patterns of child care: Some implications for service programs. In CA. Chandler, R.S. Laurie, A.D. Peters, & L.L. Dittman (Eds.), *Early child care: The new perspective* (pp. 217-236). New York: Atherton.

Coles, R. (1967). *Migrants, sharecroppers, mountaineers: Vol 2, children of crisis*. Boston: Little, Brown.

Coles, R., & Coles, J.H. (1978). *Women of crisis: Lives of struggle and hope*. New York: Delacorte Press/ Seymour Lawrence.

Cohler, B.J., & Grunebaum, H.U. (1981). *Mothers, grandmothers, and daughters: Personality and childcare in three-generation families.* New York: John Wiley & Sons.

Duberman, L. (1976). *Social inequality: Class and caste in America.* Philadelphia: J.B. Lippincott.

East Tennessee Health Improvement Council. (1984). *Health systems plan, 1984-1989* (5th ed.).

Eller, R.D. (1979). Land and family: An historical view of preindustrial Appalachia. *Appalachian Journal, 6*(2), 92, 100.

Ergood, B. (1983). Toward a definition of Appalachia. In B. Ergood & B.E. Kuhre (Eds.), *Appalachia: Social context past and present* (pp. 31-41). Dubuque, IA: Kendall/Hunt.

Fisher, S.L. (1976). Victim-blaming in Appalachia: Cultural theories and the southern mountaineer. In Ergood, B. & Kuhre, B.E. (Eds.), *Appalachia: Social context past and present* (pp. 139-148). Dubuque, IA: Kendall and Hunt Publishing Co.

Fisher, S.L. (1977). Folk culture or folk tale: Prevailing assumptions about the Appalachian personality. In *An Appalachian symposium: Essays written in honor of Cratis D. Williams* (pp. 14-27). Boone, NC: Appalachian State University Press.

Fitchen, J.M. (1981). *Poverty in rural America: A case study.* Boulder, CO: Westview Press.

Gans, H.J. (1970). Poverty and culture: Some basic questions about methods of studying life-styles of the poor. In P. Townsend (Ed.), *The concept of poverty: Working papers on methods of investigation and life-styles of the poor in different countries* (pp. 146-164). New York: American Elsevier.

Gaventa, J. (1980). *Power and powerlessness: Quiescence and rebellion in an Appalachian valley.* Urbana: University of Illinois Press.

Gecas, V. (1979). The influence of social class on socialization. In W.R. Burr, R. Hill, F.I. Nye, & I.L. Reiss (Eds.), *Contemporary theories of the family: Vol II, General theories/theoretical orientations* (pp. 365-404). New York: The Free Press.

Gecas, V. (1982). The self-concept. *Annual Review of Sociology, 8*, 1-33.

Glaser, B.G. (1978). *Theoretical sensitivity.* Mill Valley, CA: The Sociology Press.

Glaser, B.G., & Strauss, A.L. (1967). *The discovery of grounded theory: Strategies for qualitative research.* Chicago: Aldine.

Glazer, N., & Moynihan, D.P. (1963). *Beyond the melting pot: The Negroes, Puerto Ricans, Jews, Italians, and Irish of New York City.* Cambridge: MIT Press, Harvard University Press

Gochros, H.L. (1974). Sex and marriage in rural Appalachia. In F.S. Riddel (Ed.), *Appalachia: Its people, heritage, problems* (pp. 76-84). Dubuque, IA: Kendall/Hunt.

Godshalk, R.F. (Ed.). (1970). *Newport.* Newport, TN: The Clifton Club.

Goldstein, H. (1981). *Social learning and change: A cognitive approach to human services.* Columbia: University of South Carolina Press.

Heath, A. (1976). *Rational choice and social exchange: A critique of exchange theory.* Cambridge: Cambridge University Press.

Heller, P.L., & Quesada, G.M. (1977). Rural familism: An interregional analysis. *Rural Sociology, 42*(2), 220-239.

Hess, R.D. (1970). Social class and ethnic influences upon socialization. In P.D. Mussen (Ed.), *Carmichael's manual of child psychology* (Vol. 2, pp. 457-557). New York: Wiley.

Hicks, G.L. (1976). *Appalachian valley.* New York: Holt, Rinehart, and Winston.

Imre, R.W. (1982). *Knowing and caring: Philosophical issues in social work.* Washington, DC: University of America Press.

Kahn, K. (1972). *Hillbilly women.* New York: Avon.

Kaplan, B.H. (1971). *Blue Ridge: An Appalachian community in transition.* Morgantown, WV: Office of Research and Development, Appalachian Center, University of West Virginia.

Keefe, S.E., Reck, G.G., & Reck, U.M.L. (1985, March). *Family and education in southern Appalachia.* Paper presented at the meeting of the Appalachian Studies Conference, Berea, KY.

Keller, E.F. (1985). *Reflections on gender and science.* New Haven: Yale University Press.

Kephart, H. (1984). *Our southern highlanders: A narrative in the southern Appalachians and a study of life among the mountaineers.* Knoxville: University of Tennessee Press.

Kerbo, H.R. (1983). *Social stratification and inequality: Class conflict in the United States.* New York: McGraw-Hill

Kirk, J., & Miller, M.L. (1986). *Reliability and validity in qualitative research.* Beverly Hills, CA: Sage.

Kohn, M.L. (1969). *Class and conformity: A study in values.* Homewood, IL: Dorsey Press.

Leacock, E.B. (1971). Introduction. In E.B. Leacock (Ed.), *The culture of poverty: A critique* (pp. 9-40). New York: Simon and Schuster.

Lee, G.R., & Cassidy, M.L. (1981). Kinship systems and extended family ties. In R.T. Coward & W.M. Smith Jr. (Eds.), *The family in rural society* (pp. 57-71). Boulder, CO: Westview.

Levine, R.A. (1977). Child rearing as cultural adaptation. In P.H. Leiderman, S.R. Tulkin, & A. Rosenfeld (Eds.), *Culture and infancy: Variations in human experience* (pp. 15-27). New York: Academic Press, Inc.

Levitan, S.A. (1971). *Blue-collar workers: A symposium on middle America.* New York: McGraw-Hill.

Lewis, H.M., & Knipe, E.E. (1978). The colonialism model: The Appalachian case. In H.M. Lewis, L. Johnson, & D. Askins (Eds.), *Colonialism in modern America: The Appalachian case* (pp. 9-31). Boone, NC: The Appalachian Consortium Press.

Lewis, H.M., Kobak, S., & Johnson, L. (1978). Family, religion and colonialism in central Appalachia. In H.M. Lewis, L. Johnson, & D. Askins (Eds.), *Colonialism in modern America: The Appalachian case* (pp. 113-139). Boone, NC: The Appalachian Consortium Press.

Lewis, H.M., Selfridge, L., Merrifield, J., Thrasher, S., Perry, L., & Honeycutt, C. (Eds.). (1986). *Picking up the pieces: Women in and out of work in the rural South.* New Market, TN: Highlander Research and Educational Center.

Lewis, O. (1966). *La Vida: A Puerto Rican family in the culture of poverty--San Juan and New York.* New York: Random House.

Lipman-Blumen, J. (1984). *Gender roles and power.* Englewood Cliffs, NJ: Prentice-Hall.

Looff, D.H. (1971). *Appalachia's children: The challenge of mental health.* Lexington: University Press of Kentucky.

Lowe, G.D., & Peek, C.W. (1974). Location and lifestyle: The comparative explanatory ability of urbanism and rurality. *Rural Sociology, 39*(3), 392-420.

Maples, P.M. (1968). *Planning for industrialization in small communities, Newport, Tn.: A case study.* Unpublished master's thesis, University of Tennessee, Knoxville, TN.

Meltzer, B.N., Petras, J.W., & Reynolds, L.T. (1975). *Symbolic interactionism: Genesis, varieties and criticism.* London: Routledge & Kegan Paul.

Murray, C. (1984). *Losing ground.* New York: Basic Books.

Mullen, P.D. (1986). Generating grounded theory: Two case studies. *International Quarterly of Community Health Education, 6*(3), 177-214.

The new Appalachian subregions and their development strategies. (1974). *Appalachia, 8*(1), 10-27.

Newcomb, H. (1983). Appalachia on television: Region and symbol in American popular culture. *Appalachian Journal, 7*(1-2), 155-164.

Nye, F.I. (1982). The basic theory. In F.I. Nye (Ed.), *Family relationships: Rewards and costs* (pp. 13-31). Beverly Hills: Sage.

Parenstedt, E. (1965). A comparison of the child-rearing environment of upper-lower and very low-income class families. *American Journal of Orthopsychiatry, 35,* 89-98.

Pearsall, M. (1974). Communicating with the educationally deprived. In F.S. Riddel (Ed.), *Appalachia: Its people, heritage, and problems* (pp. 55-62). Dubuque, IA: Kendall/Hunt.

Petchesky, R.P. (1983). Reproduction and class divisions among women. In A. Swerdlow & H. Lessinger (Eds.), *Class, race and sex: The dynamics of control* (pp. 221-241). Boston: G.K. Hall.

Peterson, G.W., & Rollins, B.C. (1987). Parent-child socialization: A review of research and application of symbolic interaction concepts. In M.B. Sussman & S.K. Steinmetz (Eds.), *Handbook of marriage and the family* (pp. 471-507). New York: Plenum Press.

Photiadis, J.D., (n.d). *An overview of the processes of social transition in rural Appalachia.* Morgantown, WV: Office of Research and Development, Center for Extension and Continuing Education, West Virginia University.

Photiadis, J.D. (1970). Rural southern Appalachia and mass society. In J.D. Photiadis & H.K. Schwarzweller (Eds.), *Change in rural Appalachia: Implications for action programs* (pp. 5-22). Philadelphia: University of Pennsylvania Press.

Photiadis, J.D. (1986). *Community and family change in rural Appalachia.* Morgantown, WV: Center for Extension and Continuing Education, West Virginia University.

Pelto, P.J., & Pelto, G.H. (1978). *Anthropological research: The structure of inquiry* (2nd ed.). Cambridge: Cambridge University Press.

References

Precourt, W. (1983). The image of Appalachian poverty. In A. Batteau (Ed.), *Appalachia and America: Autonomy and regional dependence* (pp. 86-110). Lexington, KY: University Press of Kentucky.

Polansky, N.A., Borgman, R.A., & DeSaix, C. (1972). *Roots of futility.* San Francisco: Jossey-Bass.

Roach, J.L., Gross, L., & Gursslin, O.R. (1969). The upper, middle, working, and lower classes. In J.L. Roach, L. Gross, & O.R. Gursslin (Eds.), *Social stratification in the United States* (pp. 153-202). Englewood Cliffs, NJ: Prentice-Hall.

Roach, J.L., & Gursslin, O.R. (1969). An evaluation of the concept "culture of poverty." In J.L. Roach, L. Gross, & O.R. Gursslin (Eds.), *Social stratification in the United States* (pp. 202-213). Englewood Cliffs, NJ: Prentice-Hall.

Rosenberg, M. (1979). *Conceiving the self.* New York: Basic Books.

Schneider, D.M., & Smith, R.T. (1973). *Class differences and sex roles in American kinship and family structure.* Englewood Cliffs, NJ: Prentice-Hall.

Schwarzweller, H.K., Brown, J.S., & Mangalam, J.J. (1971). *Mountain families in transition: A case study in Appalachian migration.* University Park: Pennsylvania State Press.

Sennett, R., & Cobb, J. (1973). *The hidden injuries of class.* New York: Vintage Books.

Shutz, A. (1962). *Collected papers I: The problem of social reality.* M. Natanson (Ed.). The Hague: Martinus Nijhoff.

Smith, B.E. (1986). Women in the south: Economic survival. In H.M. Lewis, L. Selfridge, J. Merrifield, S. Thrasher, L. Perry, & C. Honeycutt (Eds.), *Picking up the pieces: Women in and out of work in the rural south* (pp. 4-5). New Market, TN.: Highlander Research and Education Center.

Smith, T. (1985, December 5). Cocke County taken to task. *The Knoxville Journal,* pp. A 1, A 12.

Spradley, J.P. (1980). *Participant observation.* New York: Holt, Rinehart and Winston.

Stack, C.B. (1974). *All our kin: Strategies for survival in a black community.* New York: Harper & Row.

Stephenson, J.B. (1968). *Shiloh: A mountain community.* Lexington, KY: University of Kentucky Press.

Tennessee Advisory Commission on Intergovernmental Relations. (1985, August). *Fiscal, economic and social profiles of county areas in Tennessee.*

Tickamyer, A.R., & Tickamyer, C. (1987a). Gender, family structure, and poverty in Central Appalachia. In *The land and economy of Appalachia: Proceedings from the 1986 conference on Appalachia* (pp. 80-90). Lexington, KY: Appalachian Center, University of Kentucky.

Tickamyer, A.R., & Tickamyer, C. (1987b). *Poverty in Appalachia* (Appalachian Data Bank Report #5). Lexington, KY: Appalachian Center, University of Kentucky.

Tulkin, S. (1977). Social class differences in maternal and infant behavior. In P.H. Leiderman, S.R. Tulkin, & A. Rosenfeld (Eds.), *Culture and infancy: Variations in human experience* (pp. 495-537). New York: Academic Press.

Tumin, M.M. (1967). *Social stratification: The forms and functions of inequality.* Englewood Cliffs, NJ: Prentice-Hall.

Turner, B.A. (1981). Some practical aspects of qualitative data analysis: One way of organizing the cognitive processes associated with the generation of grounded theory. *Quality and Quantity, 15,* 225-247.

Turner, B.A. (1983). The use of grounded theory for the qualitative analysis of organizational behavior. *Journal of Management Studies, 20*(3), 333-348.

U.S. Department of Commerce, Bureau of the Census. (1983). *1980 Census of Population, Vol 1: Detailed Population Characteristics, Tennessee.*

U.S. Department of Labor. (1965). *The Negro family: The case for national action.* Washington, DC: Office of Policy Planning and Research.

Valentine, C.A. (1968). *Culture and poverty: Critique and counter-proposals.* Chicago: University of Chicago Press.

Walls, D.S., & Billings, D.B. (1977). The sociology of Southern Appalachia. *Appalachian Journal, 4,* 131-144.

Waxman, C.I. (1977). *The stigma of poverty: A critique of poverty theories and policies.* New York: Pergamon Press.

Weeks, J.S. (1980). Is the mountain woman unique? A debate. In P.B. Cheek (Ed.), *The Appalachian woman: Images and essence* (pp. 22-26). Mars Hill, NC: The Council on Appalachian Women, Inc.

Weller, J.E. (1966). *Yesterday's people: Life in contemporary Appalachia*. Lexington, KY: University of Kentucky Press.

Whisnant, D.E. (1980). *Modernizing the mountaineer*. Boone, NC: Appalachian Consortium Press.

Wylie, R.C. (1979). *The self-concept* (Vol 2, rev. ed.). Lincoln, NE: University of Nebraska Press.

Zigler, E., & Seitz, V. (1978). Changing trends in socialization theory and research. *American Behavioral Scientist, 21*(5), 731-756.

INDEX

Abuse, *see* Physical abuse, Psychological abuse, Sexual abuse
Appalachia
   Appalachian Regional Commission, 10
   economic development, 3
   geographic regions, 10-11
   internal colonialism, 26-27
   political divisions, 10
Appalachian men, 51-57
Appalachian population
   early studies of, 6
   egalitarian ethic, 66
   families, 5, 24, 57
   mental health problems, 24-25
   personalism, 67-68
   poverty, 22-27
   stereotyping of poor, 4, 32, 33
   subculture, 22, 25
Appalachian women
   lack of statistical data, 5
   low-status, 28-29
   traditional roles, 41
Appalachian women, participants in study
   abuse of, 48, 50, 76-78
   accomplishments, 80-81
   characteristics of, 34-36
   compared to other rural women, 84
   daughter role, 48-51
   educational decisions, 59
   egalitarian beliefs, 66, 84-85
   employment of, 48, 80
   family composition, 35-36, 47, 84
   interpersonal interactions, beliefs about, 64-66
   maternal role, 42-48
   self-appraisals, 73, 75, 813, 85
   self-esteem, 74-76, 79-81
   sensitivity to feeling put down, 63, 67-71, 73, 87
   sexuality, 56
   social construction of their world, 83
   social status, view of, 61-63
   worldly experience, 58-59, 81
Battering, *see* Physical abuse
Blue-collar workers, 17
Children
   importance of, 44, 76-78
   protection of, 45, 52
   sibling rivalry, 46-47

Cocke County, Tennessee
   African-American residents, 34-35
   economic development, 33
   history of, 33
   location, 33
   media images of, 32-33
   population characteristics, 32
   poverty statistics, 33
   social stratification, 62-63
Coding, 37
Cultural Lag Theory
   Appalachians, 22-23
   individual characteristics, 23
Culture-of-Poverty Theory, 4
   Appalachians, 18, 24-25
   critiques of, 18-19, 25
   individual characteristics, 18
Daughter role, 48-51
   family loyalty, 49-50
   keeping family secrets, 50
   responsibilities, 50-51
Education
   participant's experiences with, 59-60
   reasons for dropping out of school, 50, 59-60
   in rural families, 21
Egalitarianism
   in Appalachian culture, 27
   and class behaviors, 66, 67
   ideal of, 84-85
Ethnographic method, 31-32
Father-daughter relationships, 49, 51, 52
Grounded Theory, 6
   methodology, 32
   utility of method, 86, 88
Interactional Expectations, 64-66

Low-status groups, 17
   life patterns, 17
   women, 19, 20. *See also* Social Stratification
Maternal role, 42-48
   employment, 48
   family emissaries, 45
   grandmothers, 47
   ideal mother characteristics, 44-46
   marital status, 48
   relationship with children, 46, 47, 49
   reproductive behavior, 43-44, 45
   role choices, 42, 43
   role conflicts, 48
   role failures, 57-58
Memo writing, 37
Mother-daughter relationships, 19, 46-47, 48, 50
Newport, Tennessee, 33. *See also* Cocke County, Tennessee
Parenting patterns
   Appalachians, 24-25
   found in study, 74-75
Paternal role, 51-53
   ideal father characteristics, 52
   paternity, questions of, 53
   responsibilities, 52-53
   role failures, 57-58
   step fathers, 57, 78-79
Personality Trait Theory
   individual characteristics, 23
Physical abuse
   beliefs about causes of, 56

Index

Poverty
  in Appalachia, 3, 22, 33
  rural, 21-22
  stigma, consequences of, 4
Psychological abuse, 79
Put downs, 67-71
Reciprocity, 64-66
Research
  data analysis, 36-39
  home visits, 35
  implications of findings, 86-88
  limitations of study, 39
  methods, 6, 31-32
  participants, 34-36
  purpose of study, 5, 13
  reliability, 38
  validity, 37-38
Rural areas, 11-12
  occupational roles of women, 12
Rural families
  characteristics, 20-21
  educational levels, 21
  stress, sources of for poor, 21
  women's roles, 21
Self-concept
  development of, 17
  self-appraisals, 12
  and socioeconomic class, 17
Self-esteem
  accomplishments, 78, 80
  and family role performance, 74-76
  independent thinking, 79-80
  negative feelings, 76-78
  and personal characteristics, 78-79, 81
  work outside of home, 80

Sexual abuse
  family secrecy, 49-50
  participants' experiences, 76-77
  protection from, 45-46
  step fathers, 57-58, 78
Situational Theory
  Appalachian families, 26-27
  internal colonialism, 26
  women's roles, 26
Snobby behavior, 61, 69-70
  reactions to, 85
Social construction of reality, 7-8
  view of study participants, 83
Social Exchange Theory, 64-65
  balanced reciprocity, 64-65
  generalized reciprocity, 65
Social stratification
  in Appalachia, 27, 61-63
  and egalitarianism, 27
  participants' perceptions of, 61, 64
  social classes, 9
  and social reality, 15
  stigma, 8
  and women, 10, 27
  worth/worthlessness, 28
Social work practice
  implications of study for, 86-88
Socialization
  parental influence, 16
  and social class, 15-16
  styles, 16-17
Spousal roles, 54-57
  decision making, 56
  divorce, reasons for, 55
  duties, 55-56

Spousal roles
    female loyalty, 54
    ideal mates, 54-56
    mate selection, 54
    negative behaviors, 57-58
    sexual expectations, 55-57
Structural theory
    characteristics of poor, 20
    family structure and
        function, 19
    women's roles, 19
Symbolic interactionism, 31
Theoretical sampling, 37
Theories of poverty
    cultural lag, 22-23
    culture-of-poverty, 4, 18-19,
        24-25
    psychological, personality
        traits, 23
    situational, internal
        colonialism, 26-27
    structural, 19-20
Working-class, 17